"Only my Love you need."

Dr. Rafael Gonzalez

February, 2005 St. Anthony of Padua Catholic Church:

"Lord Jesus you are my good Doctor, I had to go to the University to become one, but you understand better what a severe bilateral pneumonia, septicemia, myelodysplasia type II and shock is; the doctors weren't giving me life, but you were there, the doctors said 8 out 10 dies, but you didn't care about the statistics, you healed me and raise me up with power, I praise and love you my Lord, my House and I are yours forever," Amen.

Index

We begin in the Name of the Father, the Son and the Holy Spirit. Amen `

(Please pray)

"Forgive me Jesus I love you, I embrace your Love, I embrace the Son of God, I embrace my cross, I embrace your Kingdom and deny the world now. Amen

Superhero

When I was a child I used to pray to God:

"Please God make me superman, give me powers to defend the weak, I want to fly and be one of the good guys."

I remember having dreams of flying through the sky, but God didn't gave me super powers, nothing happened.

I had a happy childhood, despite my Father and my Mother being divorced, but it didn't hurt as much because it was a year or two after I was born; I grew up without a father at home, but my uncles took me everywhere, the afternoons eating pizza, the morning driving to the beach, the ice creams... I was happy.

I guess I was a real problem for my guardian angel (I presume), I remember being all the time climbing the mango trees and I remember one time, going to the roof of my grandma's house with a machete, a rope and a stick... bound them together and with the machete on top of the stick started to bashed the Spanish lime tree, next thing I know the machete fell in my head but only the handle struck me, not the sharp metal and I realize how lucky I was.

Luck... no... God was taking care of me, even though I wasn't praying like when I wanted to be a Superhero, eventually I got older and now (today) I realize that He did grant me my prayer, I can save the day, I can go on and squash evil with the power He has given me...

Every time I pray the Rosary evil is conquered, the monsters get punishment, the wolf gets beaten, the weak gets protected and my family shares the benefits, soon, when I get to heaven, through Jesus Mercy... I'll fly all over and share my happiness with all, as the Son of Almighty Father gave me the tool to save the day, the tool entrusted to our Lady...

I'm now a super hero of Mercy, this is why I pray the Rosary, because I love God and I want to please Him and He pleases me, as Jesus sees me and you, as the super heroes of this end times...

I feel like a child again and it is all because of you God, for seeing me through the painful wounds of your Son and letting me participate in His Mercy, by letting Him die on the cross for me, for letting Him giving me His Mother... for all of that, I thank you.

I feel like a child again and it is my only hope to please my Lord and His Mother the Queen of Heaven. Amen.

BECOME AN EX-GAY

(The heavier the cross the greater the crown)

The heavier the cross the greater the crown through Christ in heaven, the cross of an Homosexual is the most heaviest as of today... knowing Jesus Mercy and His Holy word in the bible, I wish I had such cross, but not for the reasons you are thinking...

A homosexual who has found Christ and embrace His Mercy, a Man or woman who gives their all to Jesus, is someone who wants to love Him...

By denying themselves, like Jesus wanted from ALL of us, who, like them... need to seek to be pure by denying our flesh...

The crown of those who deny themselves and embrace the cross seeking purity it is a crown so beautiful in heaven, that, this is why I say I wish I had such a cross... not as a Gay person anymore, but as a man or woman who embrace Christ, one who embrace purity by denying the flesh, and taking the persecutors fingers and suffering all the way to the Golgotha.

My cross is different than theirs, one that I constructed over the years, one that I'll carry with gladness and sometimes with tantrums...

But my cross cannot be compared with theirs, if I get to heaven, it'll be only through Divine Mercy like everybody else, but my reward and their reward is abysmal...

Heaven IS filled with murderers, adulterers, homosexuals, prostitutes, traitors, all who repented in time... all who embraced the cross of Jesus, DENIED themselves and followed Him...

Jesus doesn't CONDONE sin, many will try to make you believe otherwise... Jesus LOVES all sinners who ARE DETERMINED to embrace purity by not sinning anymore, out of their love and fear for the Lord... the strength to endure this path only will come from heaven with a YES on your part, the Lord will give you the strength to suffer those pointing fingers and once you leave this world, there in heaven, thy Crown shall be put on thy head and it'll be more beautiful, like nothing on earth...

Homosexuality is a mortal sin and whoever endures in their sin will gain eternal death, any mortal sin will make that happen on anyone... this is why Jesus said to the woman who committed adultery "Go now and LEAVE your life of sin." John 8:11

As all of us... you have to leave sin, but persevering while walking to heaven with such a stigma will gain you much in the eyes of the Lord... so, condemning is NOT our job but God's, but we shouldn't condone or encourage sin like society and some in clergy are doing today, even if a priest tells you that there is nothing wrong with such sin...

DON'T be deceived, even if you see priests with rainbow colors like those Franciscans in Boston with the "who am i to judge" banner...

RUN AWAY from them!!!

Encouragement in sin is not what Jesus wants, Jesus wants you and all of us to deny ourselves... and if you are having such a cross, Jesus will help you with the load and your crown awaits with your yes and denial of your flesh, all, right after a little crucifixion...

Judgment, pain, humiliation and suffering will come, embrace Jesus cup of suffering and your crown in heaven shall be there.

Apostle Paul was a murderer, but he beat the world with Jesus love... like you will, if you say YES.

Amen.

Guilty of His Body and Blood

Hello in Jesus Christ our Lord to whoever is reading, this an urgent advice that I hope that it pleases our Lord, this is URGENT so I will cut to the chase: The sin that almost no priest hears about, "I'm sorry father for I have sinned, because all this sins (mortal) that I've committed before, I ate His Holy flesh and Precious blood while in sin... so I'm guilty of His Blood and Holy body"

Remember what Apostle Paul said:

"So then, whoever eats the bread or drinks the cup of the Lord in an unworthy manner will be guilty of sinning against the body and blood of the Lord. Everyone ought to examine themselves before they eat of the bread and drink from the cup." 1 Cor 11:27-28

Ask yourselves: Have you ever ate His Holy flesh with a mortal sin? After progressing in your Spiritual life have you remember a mortal sin that you didn't know it was a sin but anyways you took the Eucharist? Have you ever taken the Eucharist in the hand? Have you taken the Eucharist without the proper preparation by a priest?

"For those who eat and drink without discerning the body of Christ eat and drink judgment on themselves." 1 Cor 11:29

If you haven't ever confess to a priest that you are guilty of His Holy Body and Blood, maybe is time for you to do so, ALWAYS remember to examine yourself keeping in mind that deadly sin.

And just in case you were wondering about the Eucharist in the hand, YES, it is a sin to receive in your hand the Eucharist without having open persecution declare to all Christians, even though a priest tells you is not, IT IS A SIN and I can prove it... Any time a Saint, an Angel or Jesus Christ Himself has appeared to someone and have given the Eucharist to that person, has always been in the tongue NEVER in the hand.

Remember, to examine yourselves... if you have ever been GUILTY of His Holy Flesh and precious Blood, repent and ask forgiveness through confession.

Testimony

Jesus appears to me and explained His Crown of Thorns.

I was doing the Rosary (sorrowful mysteries) and while meditating them I stopped at the Crown of Thorns, in my mind I asked Jesus "You suffered for the sins of the world in Your present and future..."

Why did you suffer specifically the Crown of Thorns?...

My surprise was huge when Jesus Himself spoke to me... I couldn't see Him but I could hear His voice as if I was talking to someone normally... I knew that He was present but couldn't see Him, only if I closed my eyes I could; He was sitting in the air floating next to me.

He said to me:
"Rafael, the Crown of Thorns I'd suffered because... All those who say that they love me, but THEY DON'T LOVE their brother."

Jesus then showed me all the times in my life that I've had the opportunity to practice charity but decided NOT to."

He showed me flashes in my life when I didn't practice charity, from NOT helping someone who dropped something on the floor and NOT helping a lady who fell to the pavement... DON'T BE LIKE ME BROTHER! Seek to be holy serving Jesus in need through your brother... It's not just being His mercy, but living Mercy through Him...

"Blessed are the merciful, for they will be shown mercy." Mat 5:7

If you serve your brother, pray for your brother and teach your brother, this are the 3 best ways to be Merciful.

The Virgin Mary in Fatima told the 3 children that most people are go to hell because NO one prays for them!

HELP, TEACH and PRAY. (Remember to pray for the souls in purgatory in your prayers).

Also remember that the Mercy of Jesus is worshipped and can be eaten. Go and participate in the Eucharist, do it today while they haven't take away the continual sacrifice (abomination of desolation Daniel 12:11).

God bless you. Amen.

Remain Faithful and RESIST!

Greetings to all of you who out there reading this words, blessings and a big hug in Jesus Christ...

Today I find myself in the same thought process as always: why should I even bother? Why should I continue to preach the words: "Watch and resist" when nobody seems to care?

My Lord in 2005 told me: "Tell the whole world about my Mercy", when I started, I began in the United States a few thousand miles from my dear Dominican Republic, I started telling people about how wrong communion in the hand is... nobody wanted to listen.

I remember starting a YouTube channel, a Gloria TV account, various blogs... but still people didn't want to listen the words, not even in my own home.

God knows my heart and He knows that my desire is NOT for people to be condemned but for them to achieve His Mercy, my sole ministry was to please my Lord, I wanted to share my testimony with the world, shout to all... that Jesus is not dead, He lives and He is God.

I've found a Church that it was off, it was bothering me more and more, people seemed to live their lives as they were already saved despite their unrepentance...

The United States... what a crazy country, seeing gays kissing each other in the streets, transgender, abortion and contraception preached in classrooms as a right and my Catholic Church omitting this type of behavior... but that's the tip of the iceberg, seeing Catholics embracing falseness was hurting.

Justice was being denied everywhere I went, when Mercy and Justice comes from the same Master... how could I turn a blind eye on that? How could I tell the world about His Mercy when seeing so much apostasy?

"There is no Mercy without Justice and Love without truth" blog came to be... the whole world embraced mindless mercy, and when I say mindless, I'm talking about NO repentance whatsoever: an automatic mercy.

No... there is no such thing... automatic mercy doesn't exist... but nobody seems to care, nobody wants to listen... this is why chastisement is coming upon this land and the kick is this: they know is coming.

My first article was how antipope Francis with his heretical exhortation opened the door to abortion, nobody cared... how many things this man have done to water down the faith and nobody cares... we see how he opens the door for Lutherans to reach the Eucharist and how condoms are preached as a 'way' to stop aids with such a poisonous words in Africa... but who cares, right?

Bergoglio IS the beast from the earth proclaimed in revelations, he is the contrast of a true pope: an antipope... and this man has poisoned the waters fulfilling St Paul in Thessalonians:

"For this reason God sends them a powerful delusion so that they will believe the lie and so that all will be condemned who have not believed the truth but have delighted in wickedness." 2 Thes 2:11-12

Read the entire 2 thes 2... we are living that chapter, but nobody cares...

It is imperative that we REMAIN FAITHFUL, and RESIST... we are living dangerous times and the easy way is appealing.

Antipope Francis has the authority to murky the waters, preaching so much poison it is just shocking and people instead of remaining firm... they embrace falseness.

Mercy without Justice doesn't exist... open your eyes, worldliness is been preached constantly and it is so easy to give in... RESIST...

The Eucharist is the target, so when the demolition becomes clearer, the Eucharist could be thrown out, so that the antichrist could come inside the Temple like a hero.

Open your eyes brethren, the la Salette prophecy is becoming true in our very noses, remain faithful and resist!

Blessings

The hope prayer

(Please pray, only when you go to sleep)

Lord Jesus, with you I lay down with you I rise up, if between them I pass away let it be in your arms, before that, forgive my sins and then, take me to heaven so I can worship in perfection Thee the Father and the Holy Spirit, fill my family with the water and blood which gushed forth from Your side, enlighten them with the light of your resurrection and seal them with the Holy Spirit, please ask your Holy Mother to cover them with Her Holy mantle, ask your Archangels to protect them from the devil, decorate them with Your Mercy now and forever .
Amen

Where was Love?

Once upon a time while dreaming I flew out the window and landed in slow motion in the ground, I remember my small airplanes shirt and the Joy of flying, but where was love in all that?

One day my Mother checked the bed and it wasn't wet for the first time, so I got a lollipop... even though I did wet a little bit after that reward, I've never did again, but where was love in all that?

We all had toys we embrace and toys we wish we had back, I remember a small helicopter given by my mother, I threw it from the 2nd floor to see what was inside, my mother was in shock and I was sad because I knew after that what was inside but the helicopter never functioned again, but where was love in all that?

I remember my first fight in middle school, a fight with a bully, it took 2 men to take me away from him, yes I won that fight and he never bully me again, but where was love in all that?

I was playing baseball, I had the bases loaded, my friends told me "hit a homer" and I replied "that's difficult to do", first pitch I saw I hit out of the park, my first homerun, but where was love in all that?

I was the clown of my class because I wanted to be accepted, I did what nobody in my classroom ever did, so I became popular, but where was love in all that?

I came out from high school as the most popular person ever, so much, that after years passed by, all my friends and teachers who were there, still call me by my nickname, yuca... but where was love in all that?

I always went out and got drunk with my buddies, my mother suffer a lot because I was wild, did liked heavy metal and always was attracted to the occult, but where was love in all that?

My university, all my friends were scared of me because they knew I could beat them up, I knew I had a bad reputation and I like it, but where was love in all that?

When I went to Medicine I was feared by my teachers, doctors and colleagues because I always had the answers, but also made the tough questions, but where was love in all that?

Once I came to know Jesus, I thought that we are saved and nothing would take away His love from me, even though I was in Church and worked in a youth group, my repentance was never there, so… where was love in all that?

Now I'm seeing clearly, that it was all self-love, as you could note in all paragraphs above, the I's and the me's; it was all self-love, I adjusted Christ love to what I've wanted it to be, I had a happy childhood but it wasn't enough, I had a tough teen years but I wanted all, I was venerated and proclaimed, but more glory I wanted… self-love the contrary to humility.

Therefore it is truly a mystery why Jesus love me so much, I didn't had one milligram of true love, nor humility and kindness for the world.

I have lied, Murdered, cheat, steal, use people, and most of all I did this while eating His flesh and drinking His blood, so I am guilty, guilty of His sacrifice… I need humility so desperately, but when I ask the Lord he says "Only my Love you need" So in time the Lord and Teacher will show me how I can be unselfish… Kind… and a victim of His.

I am not worthy, I wasn't when I first saw Him, I wasn't when He saved me from death, and I wasn't when He talked to me…

I'm still a worthless worm and I deserve hell a million times over, but he said to me "Only my Love you need" now I know where Love has been all my life... knocking at my door.

I followed self-love all of my life, a false love which is taught by the world and now I know how Paul the apostle but also the murderer felt, when that thorn of satan pinched him and Christ told him "Only my love you need"...

Tough times are ahead and the Lord has said it well "In that time, Love will grow cold"

When I was a child people use to be kind, but now everything has a price... Now everything doesn't need repentance because God forgives us automatically according to our apostate Church...

We need humility to enter heaven and that is something that is taught from heaven, you can't do it yourself, repentance first and embracing Jesus as your Lord forever must follow, trusting Him despite horror, despite the enemy, despite death.

Horror is about to fall upon whoever loves Jesus and Mary, the love that the world teaches is about to be legal and all who rejects it will be persecuted.

This is what they wanted, this is what they planned since long... people don't like martyrdom, and martyrdom is for all who despises self-love, so decide: Heaven or the world.

Heaven despite the struggles ahead, decide to be taught the depths of humility, because it'll be Humility that will open Heaven for you, loving God in secret, Loving God more than anything, Loving His plans and in His plans... there's no condoning sin, on the contrary looks to not sin... because you fear the Lord.

Blessed be God Forever! Amen

Two worlds

When I was a child I remember going to Church, to the St. Pious X chapel in Santo Domingo Dominican Republic, I had a happy childhood and it was my believe that God was in heaven and I on earth, childish stuff...

Grew up, eventually found Christ on a Saturday September 19th 1992, from that day forth, my life changed forever...

A charismatic youth coordinator, went to become part of the catechumenal Catholic Church because of my girlfriend (now wife), went to the Passionist seminary to become a priest (Yes, broke off with my girlfriend), got out and threw away the Church to become a doctor... but, I've never heard of the Latin mass.

It wasn't until I got to my 41st birthday when Michael Voris taught me that there was something called the Latin Mass, went there and from the start I felt almost in Heaven, like I just got home for the first time, the supernatural feel I've got, is exactly that... supernatural.

My call was to tell people about Jesus Mercy, but I missed my Latin Mass... my family didn't want to go so I had to go whenever I was alone... I started my ministry throughout the Church alerting people about Communion in the Hand, promoting the Divine Mercy Chaplet and how the truth was being persecuted.

Got me some Traditional friends who quickly cut all ties from me because I was a defender of the Novus Ordo Mass, my point was, if Christ is still in the Eucharist, then it is a valid mass!

Many horrible things came my way, the Divine Mercy Chaplet was being rejected by almost all traditionalists, and those in my Novus Ordo side made fun of those traditionalist minded people who I hold dear.

Caught between two worlds, Traditionalists and Neo-Catholics all rejected me...

The Catholic Church did this to herself, because it allow people to become arrogant and proud about the Bride of Christ and also let people to dismiss the truth of Holy Scripture for the sake of embracing the world.

My family don't like the Latin mass, traditionalists don't like the Novus Ordo mass where I take my family to... traditionalists are correct in one thing: <u>tradition is meant to be followed, is just that when you follow it without Love for our Lord, then we are lost</u>...

The same Happens on the other side, Neo Catholics don't follow the whole truth in Holy Scripture out of the mindset "God Love us too much that He will not throw anyone to hell"

Tradition is what we are supposed to keep, not tradition to keep us, if there's no Love for our Lord then there's only a desire to be proud and point fingers, when tradition is done with Love for our Lord, then truth is easy to see and the world cannot stand between our Love for our Lord and the Love from our Lord for us…

People need to Love our Lord, strive for Love, the Sabbath wasn't meant to chain men, in other words, the rules are in place to keep us away from evil, but without Love, then, evil has its way with us like it did with the Pharisees.

Traditionalists who Love our Lord don't point fingers and condemn people to hell, Neo Catholics who love our Lord don't laugh and make fun for those who love our Lord pleasing Him in all His commandments.

People who condemn people to hell are condemning themselves…

Two worlds, I can't be a traditionalist minded person because I'm a Neo Catholic and I can't be a Neo Catholic because I love the old way... so, I look to Holy Scripture, stand between the two and I called on to Jesus to let me Love Him in whatever way He wants in my Church... So I embrace the law, His commandments because I want to Love Him and I see what the valid post Vatican popes have done and through their teachings I Love my Lord as well.

When Jesus is Mocked and crucified again in the Novus Ordo Mass I Love Him and I pray for tears for my Lord due to His suffering; when I go to the Latin Mass, I hope and beg my Jesus to lift my heart to Almighty Father... <u>Love for our Lord is what will make us live His Glory on earth and finally do what St. Paul told us</u>...

"Therefore, brothers, stand firm and hold fast to the traditions that you were taught, either by an oral statement or by a letter of ours." 2 Thes 2:15

So Stand Firm brethren, stay faithful through Love for our Lord, His will be done and it'll be marvelous to our eyes. Amen

Walking Living Tabernacles

Five Golden Walls, the Golden gate awaits for the Key... inside there's Love, Flesh... Holy Flesh, no longer bread, no longer wheat, His Flesh, Divine Flesh... Always obeying, the source of Humility, standing at the gate to give life to those who have humble themselves through true repentance.

He awaits for hungry hearts, hearts who Love Him more than anything in this world... He stands at the gate, when the day of the Holy Sacrifice arrives, death stops, Life begins and the gates of hell are shut... no power in this world is comparable and God have chosen simplicity over complexity, by choosing Bread.

Those who wants to live forever seek the Master and Teacher and He waits for them to make up their minds... Bread, no longer bread, but Holy Flesh and Blood in a small circle of Love.

Divine Love has made it possible, Divine Love that wants to replace the Golden Tabernacle of Hope for a beating Tabernacle, a heart fill with sadness and broken dreams, once... but with true repentance, the hungry heart opens the door to He who has knock on the door since long, He who Lives forever, He who will transform your heart into the walking Living Tabernacle.

Poor those who don't know, poor those who haven't been told... it is mystery, something so small, can give you so much... yet, those who have no fault of their own, who are innocent are out there, waiting for us to proclaim the Good News.

The Living Tabernacle now have acquired legs, ears, arms and a voice... the tabernacle now has the beat of your own heart and is giving you Life, please, don't put this lamp underneath your bed, don't put it to rest, humble yourselves before Christ our Lord... shine, shine, shine in His Holy Name and proclaim Him your King to all.

You are the walking Living Tabernacle when you eat His Flesh in a state of grace...

WOE to those who proclaims otherwise, WOE to those who don't care, WOE to them who say: 'The Holy Flesh is not for the perfect', those who do... are indeed damned, you need to be in a state of Grace.

Almighty Father and I, Jesus, are one...

Once you eat My Flesh, you also get in touch with My Father... you have to be in a state of Grace and the state of grace has no arrogance, pride or hate, but a broken and humble heart through true repentance.

The impossible possible is made, all out of Love... Divine Love, so WOE to those who throw the pearl to the mud.

The Living Tabernacle is walking, in touch with the Divine, with His Holy Flesh you are Heaven around the darkness of the world... so let it shine; do not despair, do not fall away, remain firm and show it to the world.

Blessed are those who walk while been living Tabernacles, soon the grace of Joy and Hope will overpower you with your continuous perseverance, this grace will overcome any persecution, horror and death.

A drop of water will meet the ocean and that ocean is everlasting, so smile... Life within you awaits for the next sacrifice, so the flow of graces continues... smile, all of you walking Living Tabernacles.

Blessings...

What is False Mercy

False Mercy is by simple definition the contrary of Divine Mercy and Divine Mercy is love acting for us, Divine love from the offended which is God to the transgressors which is us, so... False mercy is just that, action build to deceive.

False is something that is not true, something that doesn't hold at all, is something that looks, sounds, feels or smells real but at the same time is not. When falseness combines with Mercy the definition becomes a little broader, it is a set of things, because Mercy is one thing us humans seek to heal our souls, to silence or guilt and reach out to God to welcome us back, something we need to feel at peace, it is the Light of God and without we are in darkness.

Darkness today feels normal, the world is entirely in darkness, it is run by darkness, but our souls are made in God's image and what belongs to God needs God, so when Mercy is preached immediately creates in us the spiritual urge to embrace it, as we are spiritual beings, but we are blinded by the world and by our very flesh, so False Mercy becomes attractive when we hear what our flesh wants to hear.

A homosexual who hears "who am I to judge"(1) feels relieved, their conscience goes into a "relative" peace, because they have been told all of their lives, "your behavior is wrong, wicked, the bible tells it so, homosexuality is not only a sin, but an abomination" (Lev 20:13) (2), calming people consciences are not the job of who are preaching Mercy, but to tell you the truth so you can find the light of God.

"...For this I was born and for this I came into the world, to testify to the truth. Everyone who belongs to the truth listens to my voice." John 18:37

False Mercy is what you want to hear, to relieve your conscience and that "peace" is just a lie... you see, a lie or falseness with tiny pieces of truth is a lie altogether, Homosexuality, divorce and re-married, stealing to a thief, doing borderline wrong, seeing sin as nothing, that we are all save, all of this, without true repentance is False Mercy.

When His Excellency Bishop Fellay told the world about those who preach false Mercy to people:

"...by telling them there is an open door when there is none. The door that is being opened is a door to hell! These prelates who have received the power of the keys, that is, of opening the gates of Heaven, are closing them, and opening the gates of hell." (3)

Many started helping false Mercy with the "respect" card, by not saying the truth, those who don't say the truth are harming those who belong to God, by not knowing the truth they stay in sin and after death, sin with no repentance, can open the doors of hell; truth will set you free (John 8:32) (4) said the Lord, because total truth will make you want to rethink, you either embrace the truth and repent (John 18:37) or you'll reject truth and continue in your sin.

False Mercy has the whole world and the devil protecting it with a call of bigotry, lack of understanding, sometimes calling people haters and legalists, even if you are denouncing the wicked acts, not who commits them, they say that you are judging people, when you are proclaiming the Gospel, because you are only repeating what God says and the world don't like it, hate for those who proclaim the truth.

"If the world hates you, realize that it hated me first. If you belonged to the world, the world would love its own; but because you do not belong to the world, and I have chosen you out of the world, the world hates you. John 15:18-19

But the world needs those who proclaim the Gospel to become corrupt and preach false Mercy, so many souls relax about seeking perfection and because the flesh has the urge to sin and you can't control yourself, then you sin, but with false Mercy is alright, because God "understands"... God doesn't give a law to then ignore His own law **don't be deceive**.

People want to embrace false Mercy because it gives you what your flesh needs, it calms your conscience with exactly what you want to hear, not what your soul truly needs, this is why many embrace strange teachings and many pastors are happy to give it, because they are blinded themselves out of their own sin, sin they believe don't exist or believe that God "understands" and forgives you automatically.

False Mercy is on the outside beautiful and attractive, way too easy and way too mundane... Loving the Lord is hard, following His commandments only creates enemies and pure hate from those you use to love or those who come to know you, despite that, follow the Lord and don't despair, don't hold a grudge... continue to love truth and trust the Lord.

Reject False Mercy, reject darkness, reject the devil and his works, many will say he doesn't exist but he does, and many will fight to protect him even un-knowingly FIGHT, fight, fight... your Lord Jesus is with you, nothing will harm you, even those who claim to be His apostles, preachers of falseness, look at their fruits, their bad fruits and you'll know them, false prophets (Mat 7:15-16) reject darkness, may the Lord give us the grace to repent and love Him perfectly in truth.

Amen

****

Notes:

1) http://www.nytimes.com/2013/07/30/world/europe/pope-francis-gay-priests.html?pagewanted=all&_r=0 Pope Francis telling reporters "Who am I to judge" on a Gay priest.

2) If a man lies with a male as with a woman, both of them shall be put to death for their abominable deed; they have forfeited their lives.

3) http://sspx.org/en/news-events/news/bishop-fellay-church-situation-catastrophic-5393 Bishop Fellay remarks on the Synod celebrated on October 2014.

4) "and you will know the truth, and the truth will set you free."

5) Watch out for false prophets. They come to you in sheep's clothing, but inwardly they are ferocious wolves. By their fruit you will recognize them. Do people pick grapes from thornbushes, or figs from thistles?

What is Mercy?

What is Mercy? Mercy is Divine Love in action, and this action can be seen hanging from the cross, God who was deeply offended, instead of applying His Divine Justice to all mankind, God sent His only begotten Son so the chains of sin of those who accepted Him as the Son of God, the Savior and King of Kings could be saved, Holy Blood would've been needed, so God acted... He used His Mercy, His Mercy Incarnated in our Blessed Mother' womb, Jesus Christ arrived as promise.

Mercy comes from God and He and His Son are one (John 10:30) since God is Love (1 John 4:8) and Mercy comes from Love so too Justice comes from Love... So Mercy and Justice are not divorced from one another as Love rejoices in truth (1 Cor 13:6) and what is truth? Truth is Jesus (1 John 14:6) and Truth is the very principle of Justice, so it is fair to say that Justice is also Jesus.

"Your throne, O god, stands forever; your royal scepter is a scepter for justice. You love justice and hate wrongdoing; therefore God, your God, has anointed you with the oil of gladness above your fellow kings." Psalm 45:7-8

Talking about Mercy alone is an illusion, an idea that could only be sold by the devil himself, like Mercy understands sin, that it celebrates the sinful nature of men, because God is Love and His Mercy has no bounds (which is true), like if Mercy would stop Justice forever (which is not true) once Mercy comes in Justice will also do God's will, if you repent with a true a sincere heart Mercy will be given and the grace to walk towards holiness, pain will be the result of that Justice which will sanctify us all, pain to those who have repented with contrite hearts (Hebrews 12:6-11) so this means, the repentant thief will return what was stolen and depending on the situation, a little suffering will satisfy his conversion by paying to society his bad deeds... Many examples to portray... but a little suffering coming from a little chastisement to teach righteousness, will suffice, as the Master and Teacher is Just and Merciful as He is Love.

"Divine Love from the affected (God) to the aggressor (us)" that's Divine Mercy and immediately after Justice: righteousness, taught with discipline if you are willing to follow the Lord, but if you're not, then Justice will call out for vengeance for those affected by your iniquity... This is why the most sincere call from both Mercy and Justice is:

"The Kingdom of God is at hand REPENT and BELIEVE in the Gospel." Mark 1:15

If you truly repent Mercy will be yours, if you believe, Justice will be yours, if you follow the Lord's discipline, suffering will come as your call is to be perfect as your Almighty Father is perfect (Mat 5:48) proclaiming Mercy without Justice is a mirage, an illusion... every time Jesus spoke of Mercy, afterwards He spoke of Justice the most brightest example was the Sermon of the mount as Jesus talked about how Mercy acted and How Justice acted... Jesus said 9 times blessed those who are for God and how those who are not for God, He compared them as salt without flavor:

"You are the salt of the earth. But if the salt loses its saltiness, how can it be made salty again? It is no longer good for anything, except to be thrown out and trampled underfoot. Mat 5:17

Therefore to walk towards holiness the first thing is a contrite heart asking for forgiveness, then Divine Mercy will find you, but, if you truly are contrite, you will embrace Justice and accept pain, discipline will find you, then Love and Fear for the Lord will grow... you will embrace His commandments and strive for perfection.

May you see the Lord in everything, may you rejoice in suffering out of Love for whom suffered first, may you embrace Mercy with Justice and act according to it. Amen

Say Yes, like our Most Blessed Mother Mary

Do you want to be a saint? Say yes, you need to want it, say yes like our Blessed Mother said yes, she was full of Grace, because God gave Her all the Graces, "Hail, full of Grace..." (Luke 1:28) Archangel Gabriel said...

I would like to be a saint, I'd like to say and live the most beautiful yes written in Holy Scripture, the Yes of our Most Blessed Mother Mary... all you can do?

Say yes, come Lord Jesus.

Every second, every moment our Blessed Mother kept in Her Heart our Lord's doing, She embrace His Will and cherish everything with Love, She gave herself in such a way, no wonder She is the spear of the Lord in this end times.

She will lead all those who say yes pointing to our Lord saying "Do whatever He tells you" (John 2:5), and the waters will convert to wine, the wedding shall have perfection because our Lord's wants it so... our Blessed Mother will lead the way to Her Son to those who say yes... so please, say yes.

Jesus Mother, the Woman, the vessel of Salvation in this Global flooding of darkness, is the one taking us to dry land, to Jesus...

She is the one who will crush the head of the serpent when God commands Her so, so say Yes and be in the winning team, not because you have the strength, because you know you don't have it and say Yes, come Lord Jesus.

NO saint ever have risen to sainthood without loving more than life itself the Holy Mother of God, Mary... Mary will point the way, now, do you want to be a Saint?

Say yes and follow Her instructions and you shall do the Lord's will, then you'll hear: "You have kept the good wine until now" (John 2:10)

Follow Her instructions and Scripture will be fulfill with you each time "Whoever finds me finds life and wins favor from the Lord" (Prov 8:35)... remember, the waters will turn into wine.

Many Blessings.

The three Wiseman Kings and the shepherds in the end times.

We begin by saying what happen before will happen again that nothing is new under the sun:

"What has been, that will be; what has been done, that will be done. Nothing is new under the sun." Ecclesiastes 1:9

Christmas has passed us by and we put ourselves in the line to shop the gifts, the candies, the goodies for the meals and the drinks, to celebrate Christmas when more than 2000 years ago the heavens rejoiced in another way, singing Hosanna in the highest and wishing peace on earth to men of good will, but there's a big disparity of how it was then and now... it's not what I want to talk today, it is clear that there is an abysmal difference between how we rejoice and how heaven rejoices.

Today I'm going to talk about something that no one talks about, about one meaning of the multiple meanings of the three Wiseman Kings and the Shepherds and how our world with the end times and also our love to our brothers and sisters in Christ from different denominations.

"They were overjoyed at seeing the star and on entering the house they saw the child with Mary his mother. They prostrated themselves and did him homage. Then they opened their treasures and offered him gifts of gold, frankincense, and myrrh." Matt 2:10-11

When the angels went away from them to heaven, the shepherds said to one another, "Let us go, then, to Bethlehem to see this thing that has taken place, which the Lord has made known to us." "So they went in haste and found Mary and Joseph, and the infant lying in the manger." Luke 2:15-16

They all went there and found our King, I could see all of them throwing themselves to the ground trying to worship God in the flesh... now, see there's no difference between them shepherds and Kings, when they are worshiping the Lord, they all adore Him and their love was accepted as men in adoration to our Lord Jesus, even though there is a clear distinction amongst them.

Then John said in reply, "Master, we saw someone casting out demons in your name and we tried to prevent him because he does not follow in our company." Jesus said to him, "Do not prevent him, for whoever is not against you is for you." Luke 9:49-50

This three Wiseman Kings and the many shepherds symbolizes in our world today, The Catholic Church, The Orthodox Church, The Coptic Church, the messianic Jews and the many protestants churches, all those who love Jesus with all their hearts and adore Him humbly like in that time, their adoration IS accepted.

Now before you get scandalized and start shouting heresy left and right considered this words with the light of wisdom of the Holy Spirit.

Extra Ecclesiam nulla salus in which states "outside of the church there's no salvation."

Now am I saying that this is wrong? NO... it is not wrong, now I'm I saying that everybody who loves Christ and follow His precepts in the other CHRISTIAN Churches will go to hell, of course NOT!

The Truth is that there's NO division in heaven, TRUTH is that the Catholic Church here on earth is a GIFT from Almighty Father, TRUE that Ecumenism is a tool of the devil to demise and destroy the Catholic Church, for me TRUE Ecumenism is when everybody accepts Catholicism hands down... BUT, how can we deny those who have given their lives for the gospel in places where the Catholic Church didn't reach, how can we denied those who don't know about schism and have embrace Jesus Mercy?

Those who are amongst those 105,000 Christians killed each year... YES there's a lot of errors in what some teach, YES there is many who profess iniquity in their ranks, YES they have half-truth and even some, open the doors of HELL for you to fall in it, but do NOT fall in the same mistake the Pharisees did because they thought of themselves as saints walking on earth (John 9:40-41), there are things in the doctrine that are NOT dogma but because it is the Church, we accept the teaching as infallible even though they're not and the Church doesn't say they are...

Remember at the beginning? Ecclesiastes?, when it says "What has been, that will be; what has been done, that will be done. Nothing is new under the sun."

A star preceded them until they found the child, the angels told the Shepherd about the Messiah and they all Adore Him with all their hearts, out of ALL the humans in the world, three Wiseman pagans and many Jewish Shepherds went before Him, this is in the beginning of the Gospel, the arrival of salvation here on earth and this STAR precedes all three Churches to Him and the angels lead them to the Child which had the STAR as a marking spot of Salvation.

ALL Churches will be ONE in adoration someday, more sooner than you think, as THE GREAT SIGN WILL APPEAR IN THE SKY (Rev. 12:1) and all humanity will see the SIGN of the CROSS like the STAR they saw then and humanity will fall to the ground like the Wiseman DID and ADORE AS ONE BEFORE THE EYES OF THE LORD.

The Great sign foretold in Garabandal is just on the corner, and when this happens many WILL cry because of our dark souls; it doesn't matter if your Jewish you will believe, it doesn't matter if you're Christian you will believe, it doesn't matter if you're Coptic you will believe, it doesn't matter if you're Orthodox you will believe, it doesn't matter if you're Catholic you will believe, a seer has been telling for more than 3 years now that this generation has been chosen to receive this Great miracle of Love, not because of our virtues, but because of all the EVIL in the world amongst ourselves.

NO there's no heresy here, all of us shall become one with the Catholic Church, not the apostate Church, but the Remnant Church, now I'm I saying don't evangelize them? Of course NOT!

Bishop Sheen said: 'the Catholic Church is a gift of Almighty Father' and because we love our brothers, we want them to have the loveliest gift: Catholicism, we want them to have the sacraments...

Michael Voris has a set of DVD's called "where the bible came from" which explains the origins of the bible and attacks the error, not the ones who committed them (That's what we need to do, denounce the error).

Now, if you haven't pray for all other faiths to embrace Jesus Mercy, start my brothers and sisters, if you haven't start praying for this clergy who embrace false ecumenism and wants to sell the Church for 30 coins, please pray even harder...

Times are rough up ahead, as we entered in more dark times as many today, the clergy thinks that the Church is better than ever, when the flock is literally on fire due to confusion.

We shall become one to adore Him in Spirit and truth, a sign in the sky will soon lead the way, pray daily the Divine Mercy Chaplet for all Christians around the world, pray for all sinners so they could accept and embrace forever the Mercy of Jesus, as the sign is very soon to show in the sky.

May Jesus Keep you in His open side throughout this dark times and the upcoming tribulation of the Church. Amen.

Few against many

I am speaking the truth, not one single word deviates from it and I stand by this words with my life.

Every step of the way, throughout the whole bible... Few stood their ground, Few stood against many, Few won, out of their love for the Lord, this is the story of the Church.

Read the bible, from left to right, up and down... only a FEW simple men did saw the warning signs, saw how the top corrupted itself and how the top preferred to follow the world...

FEW simple men preferred to obey God rather than men (Acts 5:29).

90% of the Catholic world has embrace some sort of EVIL in one way or another: Contraception, Abortion, Homosexuality, you name it... apostasy has been running wild since long, growing bit by bit until an 'accelerant' was placed on top.

Back in memory lane... few stood with Samuel, only a few stood with Moses, St Athanasius stood against 99% of all the Catholic world who embraced Arianism, 11 disciples started the Catholic Church, and Peter was rebuked by St. Paul and thanks for his rebuking, Peter came back to his senses.

Didn't Caiaphas when Jesus was alive, represented God back in the day as His prince? Didn't Caiaphas throne represented the hand of God on earth? Did Jesus stood silence against the top in those days? On the contrary Jesus didn't had nice words for them...

"You belong to your father, the devil, and you want to carry out your father's desires. He was a murderer from the beginning, not holding to the truth, for there is no truth in him. When he lies, he speaks his native language, for he is a liar and the father of lies." John 8:44

Caiaphas and the Pharisees didn't repent and Jesus was killed. Today one Billion plus Catholics cheers ambiguous mercy and only a few around the world have seen this, the same thing the FEW back then saw: APOSTASY.

Apostates are hiding behind authority and tons of ambiguity with the most beautiful words... Mercy and respect for people's consciences, respect in regards to give up what is sacred.

Our lady said it in La Salette, "Rome WILL lose the faith and becomes the seat of the antichrist"

We are seen the top preaching mindless mercy, NO repentance preached and anyone who dare to say anything about it, are treated as demons and enemies of the Church.

We are seen the same thing that happened in the past, same thing it happened throughout the history of the Church, FEW are standing by God's law, few against many... and this many are in power, clergy and laity of this few... are being maligned.

Cardinal Sarah is being persecuted already for rejecting this synod, Poland is seen as schismatics by rejecting this wicked synod, and those who dare to say, that the top is the one at fault by his omissions and ambiguous poison, are treated as Jehovah witnesses.

The same happened with Samuel, with Moses, with St Athanasius, St Benedict, St John of the cross, St Hildegard and Jesus... they were called demons and false.

But they all stood their ground, remained by God's law and they all prayed for those who lost their way... so we too have to pray for their souls.

It is my sincere hope that God open your eyes, there is still time...

Sooner or later, the antichrist will waltz inside the Holy Temple and in order for the antichrist to come in, the Temple must be corrupted by the help from within and like Caiaphas and Judas did, what is sacred will be cast away for the sake of abomination.

FEW nowadays are called saints, few saw apostasy when many saw falseness presented as heaven... today is the same, today we try show the lies presented as truth and we are called Demons and legalists...

Thank you Jesus for letting us suffer for the sake of the Kingdom at hand, please forgive them and let them come back to your side before apostasy allows the antichrist to seat in the Holy Temple with the help of those on top. Amen

Manger

(Luke 2:12)

Our Savior came, the owner of all Glory...

The King of Kings incarnated, and a star was shining,

The Holy Angels proclaimed His arrival

And the shepherds went to adore, the Wiseman Kings arrived with presents

To Honor the Lord of Lords...

The most beautiful scene feasted their eyes,

Eyes of unworthy pastors and kings

When they saw what prophets of old never saw,

The promise Messiah has arrived

And the Heavens rejoiced...

The owner of all Glory, laid in a manger...

A manger for animals to eat,

He who owned the complacencies of Almighty Father...

Has incarnated as poor of the poorest,

They marvel on how God love, those who have nothing but His love...

The Manger of Love, humility, Joy and Obedience...

All the Universe saw the will of The Father and they marveled...

His only begotten Son, the King of Glory, placed in a Manger.

May we come to adore and say Like St. Francis of Assisi once said while recreating the nativity...

"All towns are Bethlehem." Amen.

The Eucharist mockery

I never seat in the firsts seats in my Church during mass, I don't like being watch by the whole congregation as I walk in to participate in mass, I got curious, in my mind I ask the Lord: "Why am I seating here Lord, do you want me to see something?" Hold that thought for a second.

Since the beginning of the History of Salvation you can see how a spotless lamb was used for the sacrifice in the Holy Temple, also the blood put on the dintels of the Jews doors to avoid the darkness that killed every Egyptian first born, God from day one reminded the chosen people, a spotless sacrifice would chase away darkness.

A spotless lamb, which if we remember Holy Scripture, our Lord was taken like a lamb to be slaughter, and how a lamb behaves taken to the slaughter house? No resistance, that is exactly how it happened, much violence on Him, slaps, spats, punches, severe blows to His precious body, the pain, the blood and the chunks of Holy flesh slashed away from violence.

Jerusalem was bathed in His Holy blood, the Pretoria and the streets with pieces of flesh everywhere, His precious Flesh dropped by violence, down on the ground...

Now, back to that thought... I sat down while mass was happening, my mind had that question circling around: "Lord, I never seat here... what do You want me to see?"

The procession to receive communion began, I watched and I see many taking the Lord in their hands, but this usher came, took Jesus in his hands and after eating Him, walked away cleaning his hands like they were dirty, like when we had our hands with dust or dirt and you need to clean them...

The particles, the Holy particles, the Holy Flesh thrown to the ground like it happened 2000 years in Jerusalem, this is just how today communion in the hand has been the biggest mockery to Jesus, an "allowed" sin.

Spiritual people out there, they see this mockery as horrific and sinful, you just know this is true because ALL THE SAINTS WHO HAVE RECEIVE MIRACULOSLY THE EUCHARIST BY JESUS, THEY NEVER RECEIVE THE HOLY HOST IN THE HAND ONLY IN THE TONGUE, so the Church allowed this and God permitted this for the chaff and the wheat to be separated.

The Novus Ordo, the new mass is not evil because bread is still being transformed into Holy Flesh out God's Mercy, but this passion, has been allowed, so that the enemies of God could be drawn out and those, who say they love the Lord, show if they really Love Him.

Years ago I use to take the Eucharist in the hand, thanks to God's Mercy, not anymore; there are many people out there, that just don't know this evil and many Judas are calling the flock to be afraid of germs and prohibiting Communion in the tongue citing illness, germs and hygiene... Ebola, measles... is all a mockery, mockery from satan through his puppets.

Pray, pray, pray... pray for our priests, their being attacked by demons to surrender to the world, the truth is being mocked and ridiculed, darkness is here my brethren, the Catholic Church is taking the hit from the serpent to its heel and the top nowadays is cheerfully helping.

If you Love the Lord don't take part in this new beating of Him, don't take the Eucharist in the hand, kneel if you can, and don't let them take your right to receive the Eucharist in the tongue, Cardinal Arinze has given light on this: "Communion in the hand is the exception NOT the rule"

Our forefathers have said that Communion in the hand was only allowed under **open persecution** and the Church was persecuted since day one until Constantine made Catholicism the religion of the Roman Empire, **so there's no more open persecution**.

Don't be deceive, although the new mass is allowed and it is valid, the Eucharist is suffering mockery, don't be a part of that, Jesus is receiving the mockery today like He did in Jerusalem 2000 years ago, but He doesn't turn away from it, so you too don't turn away, receive the Eucharist in the tongue while kneeling and if they humiliate you or rebuke you, receive those punches and offer it to Jesus, the Eucharist is Holy and won't give you Ebola or measles, if you are spiritual you know it.

Blessings.

Bergoglio teachings

Today I reach out to our Lord, took the Holy Bible and read Luke 21:8 that says...

"He replied: "Watch out that you are not deceived. For many will come in my name, claiming, 'I am he,' and, 'The time is near.' Do not follow them."

As we try to open eyes across the Catholic World, the top continues to preach confusion, but people prefer to ignore us.

Mario Bergoglio when got elected did claim in one of his speeches that he hoped that people would claim "that's not a man, that's Jesus"... we know that each priest represents Jesus, but constantly deny His teachings? Has been shocking.

The problem is not that Mario Bergoglio is who he is (The false prophet), the problem is Catholics dealing about embracing someone with blind obedience, despite his ambiguity.

BLIND OBEDIENCE for men is a problem, if there's wickedness on the commands they obey, each and every act of pure hate and crime against good men has come from lies, hate and most were due to omission.

OMISSION is what is eating up Catholics today hiding under the flag of obedience, IF St. Paul wouldn't have rebuked Peter, he would've condemn himself. (Galatians 2:11)

"When Cephas came to Antioch, I opposed him to his face, because he stood condemned."

Bergoglio has said plenty of things that are heretic but most people prefer omission instead of truth... being obedient is an act of Love, and we MUST obey God rather than men (Acts 5:29)

Doctor of the Church St. Bellarmine and most forefathers of the Church have taught that we shouldn't follow wolves in sheep clothing, but instead resist them and see that their commands don't come to fruition, but Catholics prefer to turn a blind eye because they don't want to CHANGE their way of life.

One of his "teachings": Denying that Jesus didn't multiply the bread and fish when he said:

"I would like to share about the bread and fish, that, they didn't multiply, it is NOT true, they simply didn't end, like the flour and oil of the widow didn't end... it wasn't MAGIC"

Bergoglio has preached tons of falseness, all forefathers have taught: the multiplication of the bread and fish DID happened, that it was an ACT OF POWER...

The Nazis obeyed, the red army obeyed, Isis is obeying a false religion and what happened? Horror happened, few broke away from the lies and embraced truth... ASK YOURSELF THIS:

In the whole History of Salvation, how many times FEW EMBRACE TRUTH and almost the entire world FOLLOWED THE EASY WAY... THE LIES!!! All through the bible that's what happened, now... What are you following?

Jesus did taught, that FALSE PROPHETS WILL HAVE PLENTY OF BAD FRUITS and Bergoglio has miles of bad fruits from Argentina to Rome... St Francis of Assisi said that many will prefer to reject truth instead of objecting error due to obedience.

Bergoglio has insult orthodoxy, have taught pure shady stuff, tell me... IS OUR LORD A LIAR?

BECAUSE IF HE DIDN'T MULTIPLY WITH HIS DIVINE POWER THE BREAD AND FISH AS BERGOGLIO CLAIMS, THEN HIS DIVINITY IS IN QUESTION... but, I'm sure that many Jews are happy with that "teaching."

OPEN YOU EYES, Bergoglio have claim that his homilies, exhortations, etc... are "teachings", which have relax souls and fall back in a false pillow of obedience, NAZIS DID THE SAME and horror followed suit, WAKE UP.

There is a pope alright, but he is suffering for the Church... sweet pope Benedict XVI, who was opposed, maligned, pushed out and dismissed... All who contradicted and disobeyed him are the same ones who are proclaiming obedience to a false pope, we are witnessing the demolition... and it is our job to wake up and rebuild ONLY through Jesus Commands.

"If you love me, you will keep my commandments" John 14:15

OPEN YOUR EYES...

Blessings.

TRUTH WILL GET YOU CRUCIFIED. (Card. Burke's Calvary)

For anybody who haven't noticed...

'Bishop against Bishops, Cardinals against cardinals... Rome will lose the faith...'

Has the prophecy been fulfilled? Do we need more? Because it will only get worse... Nowadays we can't give way to lose heart as Apostle Paul said clearly in 2 Thes 2: 'the apostasy needs to come first and the man of perdition to appear'

Is like in the days of Noah and Lot, said the Lord, and those days were going to be shortened for the sake of the elect... Franciscans parading on gay parades, Bishops upholding the truth been humiliated and demoted, laity cheering the demotion as a good thing, because everything that comes from our hierarchy is viewed as 'holy'.

Families torn apart, separated from one another, if one looks to be holy through our Lords Mercy then that person is an extremist, fanatic and if he or she sees apostasy and denounce it, then they're not catholic, they're sinners of the worst kind, worse than satanists... Our own faith has taught us, 'TRUTH WILL GET YOU CRUCIFIED'

Look how many around here applauds everything coming from the hierarchy, ask yourselves this, were are they when ORTHODOXY suffers? This Bishop is a good man, a man of truth, a man who just started his own Calvary, now where are this people? They're not here offering a prayer, and if they are, they target the news with a post worthy of Lombardi or put some senseless commentary about respect, respect to the most holy pope that has ever seated in Rome, someone who is viewed today more holy than the apostles themselves because the things he says and does (even if they go totally contrary to what Jesus said), are beyond holiness than anyone else before.

Pope pious XII IGNORED but John XXIII a saint? Pope St Pious X totally ignored, and Walter Kasper is doing theology while kneeling, Muslims chanting against the infidels in the Vatican, and the Motu propio from Benedict and all his legacy destroyed... where are this people who venerates, cheers and views ORTHODOXY as mad trads?

It is not our duty to follow men who constantly embraces worldliness and ambiguous false mercy... my lesbian sister, I was reminding her of Jesus and how she needed to embrace Christ while seeking chastity and she said to me 'your pope has declared live and let live... why don't you renounce heterosexuality like your telling me to quit lesbianism, live and let live'

So I will say this again, we can't follow wolves in sheep clothing, we CAN'T stay silent; Cardinal Burke, Bishop Livieres, and that African UN bishop who did Latin mass in NY are out, most simple priests who speak truth are being silenced by the Bergoglian police... where are this people who like to cheer? Where are they? The Franciscans of the immaculate are down to their knees and who is praying for them?

Bishop Sheen, a woman came to him and said 'I don't believe in hell' and he replied 'Don't worry you'll believe when you get there', most of the people who don't question anything but cheer, those are considered normal, but those who don't like the Kool aid and questions everything, those are fanatics.

TRUTH AND ONLY TRUTH WILL SET YOU FREE, IT WILL GET YOU CRUCIFIED and crucifixion is heaven in a silver platter; smile Jesus is coming soon. Amen.

CRYING I LOVE YOU JESUS

(I was crying when I wrote this as me and my wife talked divorce and Jesus comforted me.)

I'm writing this words with my heart broken, my tears rolling down my face like I'm 5 years old again, looking back to where I was in life, where am at and where I want to be... I was in a very difficult situation when I graduated in Med School, I was top 5 among my peers, at the time not even the number one student could've had a brighter future than mine, I was the type of person who corrected professors in their own field of medicine, I was the type of students that when a question was asked the whole classroom turn to me like it was a cartoon and I had the answer, if they had a survey about who was the most likely person to succeed in life I would've been the # 1 choice.

I was on the move to take over the world when I got ill during my pediatrics internship, after severe pneumonia, shock, acute kidney failure and atrophy of my bone marrow I was about to die, on January 4th 2005 and later on the 8th due to a relapse, I was in coma the whole time... people all around the world started to pray for this young Doctor even inside the hospital that I was in; two different people saw Jesus Christ beside my bed taking care of me and after I woke up His Mercy was so great that I thought it only passed a day sleeping... I woke up, not been able to talk, walk, I had to be dialyzed every now and then. After I came out knowing that I was saved through a miracle... I had to go to the United States for surgeries because I had a tracheal stenosis and couldn't breathe, after more than 15 surgeries I lose count and the end of 2008 I was recovered but... with 60% of trachea function a permanent tracheostomy (an opening between the trachea and the skin).

Thanks to God by His sweet Mercy He preserved my vocal chords, because the mass which obstructs my trachea up to 40% makes it difficult to lose sound, Thanks my Lord! After the years I couldn't go back to medicine because I had an open door to infections (tracheostomy).

In 2005 Jesus appeared to me in a dream and told me to speak to the world about His Mercy, His Mercy is the arms and legs of Love running to those who embraces His sacrifice for them, but the thing about Mercy is that you can't speak about it without Justice in the room... if Mercy are the arms and legs then Justice is the chore where this arms and legs are attached... There is NO MERCY WITHOUT JUSTICE and NO JUSTICE WITHOUT MERCY... Mercy alone is an illusion.

His Justice was applying on to me when I was ill... you see, I used to do God's work, I used to evangelize people, been in the church and even went to the passionist seminary to try and become a priest... but I preferred the world, got out from the seminary, got married, started a family, had 3 beautiful children, went to med school, got ill, graduated while i was having my surgeries and all of that was a good thing in the eyes of the world (except ill part), BUT... I forgot God on the way, I mean... I put God in the last place of my life when I used to go to Him telling him that he was # 1, having a family is a wonderful thing, a blessed thing and I have never regret not been a priest ever, I would've been a terrible one... I forgot God, put the world first and the thirst for its fruits.

Now years later I have a modest job, trying to spread the word every now and then with my beautiful family on my back and the thirst for Jesus greater than ever. When I started to spread Jesus Mercy I started attacking Communion in the hand... what happened? My family didn't want to hear about me talking about God anymore in my own house!.. I gave my testimony in my Church and what happened? At the beginning all cheered and praise God, now?

I'm a 'know it all' and a lunatic... even my priest won't speak to me anymore! I started preaching God in my job bit by bit and what happened? I was reprimanded and told not to pray the rosary again in my own time! I started to tell all about the mercy of God in Gloria.tv teaching what God likes and doesn't like (Atheists to heaven, Jesus pretended, Mary felt cheated and the heretic Evangelii Gaudium) what happened? They called me protestant, schismatic, vomit, antichrist, and lefebvrist...

God through me called all of you for a sacrifice of prayer in which a 24 hour of Mercy chaplets are called on the 22nd in which you could pray for life whatever amount of chaplets you feel you could do to help us (but 24 is the goal)... and what happened the day after that was called? My wife and I are separating...

Do you think that I have come to establish peace on the earth? No, I tell you, but rather division. From now on a household of five will be divided, three against two and two against three; a father will be divided against his son and a son against his father, a mother against her daughter and a daughter against her mother, a mother-in-law against her daughter-in-law and a daughter-in-law against her mother-in-law." Luke 12:51-53

My heart is broken... yes, am in pain... yes, I look back and I see my indifference... yes, I see all that have gone through...yes, I see the hearts of the faithful blind to the word of God in this NEW WORDLY CHURCH... yes, but my tears are rolling because God's love doesn't forsake me, Jesus is here with me as I'm writing you my brothers in Christ and it is my wish that He makes you and me His, forever...

May the two Lights of Mercy which cones out of Jesus heart be your guide and may Jesus comes and take all of us with Him to see and live the Father for eternity. Amen

Benedict in silence

We can't blame Benedict for what the Church slowly has become, he tried to correct in some ways a deadly and wrong perception of Vatican II, in which almost all Bishops failed, the Latin mass was never canceled.

Catechism is clear we shouldn't hate people, but rather out of love tell them the truth, sodomy is a grave sin and because we respect you, we are not condoning anything, because the world condones you and celebrates your sin, the Catholic Church with the truth at hand must tell you that God loves you and forgives you, but you should pursue conversion and purity.

The same is with all clear teaching like divorce and re-married, you are welcome to the Church but you need to embraced and pursue conversion, have only spiritual communion.

Clear teaching from the apostles handed down to us and in 2000 years nothing have change, no dogma has change and it is also clear that dogma can't be modify, erased or forgotten if you truly love the Lord.

Benedict knows what is going on, he is one of the brightest minds of the Church and he has prophesied all of this since the beginning:

'Pray for me, that I may not flee for fear of the wolves." Benedict XVI.

Then after the scandals, the defrocking of many priests (more than 400 - who abused the innocent), the "whoever is a homosexual cannot be a priest", the "Islam is not a religion of peace", Vatileaks, the overall disobedience by his bishops, the constant false and wicked PR from the secular media pushing him to resign, but the Vicar of Christ prepared the flock... the year of faith.

It wasn't a coincidence, the "Whoever thinks Fatima has ended is wrong", the "Church will become small", the "I'll be with you even though I will remain hidden from the world" plus the year of faith, was all a preparation for what is about to unfold...

Apostasy! (2 Thes 2)

Benedict XVI, a true pope, a martyr, my friend and holy father has suffered and still is, his pains are the offering to our Lord Jesus for the Church, praying for all, his enemies and those like me who never pray for him, who didn't like him and now after giving oneself to Jesus (finally), see my mistakes and embraced the Vicar of Christ like I should've done from the beginning.

Benedict has been seen around Francis, attending in some capacity to some Church events, but hasn't condemned Francis publicly, his silence has been loud as he is praying and watching... you see, he can't say anything because in his mind there is NO definitive act of heresy yet, all is smoke and more smoke.

Benedict is waiting fire, not simply some prophecies here or there, no... Remember he is the pope and as pope he needs something definitive and this synod shall give this to him, next October you shall see what a true Vicar is made of... the small Church is set after 2015, and it is not a new Church, but the same Catholic Church in the wilderness, not with structures, but with faith.

Blessings.

The Wilderness (the desert)

"Then another sign appeared in the sky; it was a huge red dragon,... Its tail swept away a third of the stars in the sky and hurled them down to the earth. Then the dragon stood before the woman about to give birth, to devour her child when she gave birth. She gave birth to a son, a male child, destined to rule all the nations with an iron rod. Her child was caught up to God and his throne. The woman herself fled into the desert where she had a place prepared by God, that there she might be taken care of for twelve hundred and sixty days." Rev 12:3-6

The Wilderness, the desert... the place we must flee when the time is right, most people find it hard, most people think this is some legend, story or science fiction thing, a thing created in the imagination of a man named John.

Those who have faith and love the Lord must not be afraid, the Catholic Church, like it happened to Israel in the Beginning, was persecuted, imprisoned, martyred... soon all the prophecies within revelations will start to come true in our very faces, and most of us, out of lack of understanding, will not be prepared.

What's in the desert? A desert doesn't have riches, fruits, or vegetation... it's even hard to find water there, our Lord suffer 40 days without food living in caves, around bushes, with cold, heat, no food or water. Sure He is God, but He lead by example and soon, like St Athanasius did, we will live in exile with no structures, only with faith.

In the desert Jesus had His Father and suffered all mentioned above, we will too have The Holy Trinity but, it's the desert... no structures!

When Lot came out of Sodom and left anything he once knew he didn't look back, when Noah closed the door of the Arch he didn't look back... So we too must not look back, so... when we must Flee?

"When you see the desolating abomination spoken of through Daniel the prophet standing in the holy place, then those in Judea must flee to the mountains, a person on the housetop must not go down to get things out of his house, a person in the field must not return to get his cloak. Woe to pregnant women and nursing mothers in those days. Pray that your flight not be in winter or on the Sabbath." Mat 24:15-18

When this desolation takes place? When those who have treasured the truth of the Gospel for thousands of years rejects the truth for their own satisfaction, when total apostasy is placed and total mockery of the Holy Sacrifice makes the Lord Flees the Eucharist from this false Church (2 Thes 2:7)

Many in the Catholic Church has done so already, not by creating another Church, but remaining faithful (like it happened with the SSPX), but when the doors of Hell are opened for men, those on top telling them sin is ok and normal, that God understands our sinful nature and legalized sin, that's when we need to Flee...

Note those words...

"A person in the field must NOT return to get his cloak back" A person in the "field" and "cloak"... PRIESTS, once in the field, after total apostasy, those who love the Lord must NOT return where the cloak is, the false church will held you captive and will make you fall, those in the rooftops, those, who are spiritual don't need to get anything, ruin and destruction will follow those in that time who, like the unprepared virgins, go out and seek oil... the false Church will lead you stray and then it'll be too late, the doors will shut, Sodom will be surrounded by destruction...

Once Apostasy is set there's nothing for you to do but remain faithful, there's NO more time... Persecution will follow, but remain faithful, Horror must follow, but remain faithful... Private revelation has given us many warnings, once apostasy is set... FLEE and no turning back until Jesus return.

Remain watchful, remain faithful, FLEE at the right time so your reward could be greater, after Apostasy the man of perdition will be revealed and the real persecution will make many martyrs and martyrdom is heaven in a silver platter. Amen

Poland: The Land of Martyrs

Greetings my brethren of Poland, it is my hope that this words get to you, a big hug in Jesus Christ...

You are courageous indeed, if there is a land on this earth that I would've like to live in, it is in yours, the Land of Martyrs, the Land of the New Disciple John, Pope John Paul II the Great in the words of our sweet Christ on earth, Benedict XVI.

The Land of Martyrs, because with your blood our dear Catholic Church received plenty of renewal and God Almighty gave the new John, pope John Paul II the great... our dear Father Pio saw a pope before there was a pope, saw someone who was willing to take the red beast by the Horns and in the Name of our Lord, pull it out from your hearts.

It is with sadness that I have to tell you that the secret sect have consumed the Eternal city and the confusion is flowing under the flag of ambiguity.

This past Synod was constructed to serve the devil and it did please their evil master, beforehand, this Synod had everything made out to destroy sound doctrine, and those free masons when stopped, had to go to a plan "B" relatio, in which they proclaim the very words of Darkness...

"It is not a blanket "yes or no" to Communion for the divorced and remarried, but a call to careful discernment." pure hellish words when Matthew says...

"Let what you say be simply 'Yes' or 'No'; anything more than this comes from evil." Mat 5:37

Jesus with His Holy eyes looked how this people served their master well, the devil... Jesus kept praying and praying while His Sweat fell like Blood in the ground, out of this so called "disciples" who are supposed to know better, but instead have chosen the path of Judas.

Jesus children reach out to Him, with a yes like our Holy Mother did to God through Archangel Saint Gabriel, like sweet pope John Paul II the Great did to our Lord, a yes of SUFFERING, a yes of fear and tremble to achieve salvation, Jesus Children says NO to the World and the devil.

This Synod have embraced the World, have embrace the devil, have weakened the family, have humiliated those who have chosen to live their lives in chastity, by living as brother and sister ALL out of their love for Christ.

Those Communists that trample your Land, they obeyed their superiors, they obeyed satan and his fallen angels, like those nazi soldiers did, obeying lies creates much horror and those who trust the Lord suffers much in Martyrdom.

Many Saints and Martyrs came out of your Land, many did embrace apostasy and lies too as they didn't want to suffer, so instead of courage they became cowards.

The Land of Martyrs then, the Land of Courage Now and the Land of suffering next...

In the end, Martyrdom have never left you... the antichrist does not forgive and his puppets are plotting against you now, as the disciples of this New John have drawn a line in the sand with the Catholic right to resist evil.

No pope has the power to change doctrine, neither change the practice a true pope would've condemned this Synod back in 2014... a true pope. They are twisting John Paul the great words to achieve their goals, please... don't flinch, stand firm and stay faithful.

Pray for His Excellency Arch. Stanislaw Gadecki and all the clergy there, their persecution has doubled in the invisible world and in Rome.

DO NOT FEAR, have no fear... in the very words of sweet pope John Paul II the Great, this was foreseen, the final battle between the true Church and the Anti-church did started long ago, but they (the anti-church) have taken over, and it is time to raise our Rosaries in obedience to God... NOT in obedience of men.

Stay faithful my Brethren, do NOT fall away from the Bride of Christ, embrace the 2000 years of traditions taught by our forefathers, do NOT flinch, even if they flash pope John Paul's words in a wicked context to filled their needs... RESIST!

The son of perdition does not forgive, so much blood will be spilled next... are you ready sweet Poland? Are you ready to embrace Martyrdom out of Love for your Lord?

Martyrdom, heaven in a silver platter... my only wish is that I could be there with you, to get martyred with you, pray those Divine Chaplets, get to the Sacraments and recite the Holy Rosary for the Catholic Church and your pastors, because the secret sect have taken over the buildings... but we have our faith!

Blessings...

Prayer

(The wedding of Cana prayer, please pray)

"Oh Mary conceived without sin pray to your Son our Lord Jesus Christ to change the waters of our lives into another color, turn Lord Jesus like you did in Cana the waters of our lives into wine, so our lives could have another color, the color of your Love."

Open Letter to Michael Voris

Dear Michael, I saw a vortex in which you defended the way the washing of the feet it's supposed to be, how you blasted all this priests washing the feet of children, woman, etc... And you went further by adding the document (stop the mandatum abuse) which defends the washing of the feet as a ritual only by priests and for priests no one else, but even though I find strange how you stayed quiet when the pope washed the feet of Muslims and a woman... not even a word defending the truth.

http://www.youtube.com/watch?v=BMCjp8JI44A

Then you started to blast the media about the twisting of the words of Francis to fulfill their agenda, as there was a worldly frenzy about the pope being all inviting with Gays, abortion and contraception...

Now where were you when the Bishop of Rome said that the church can't interfere with the spirituality of Gays? Where was any vortex being made about Evangelii Gaudium n.252 backing all Muslims and the **profound veneration to Jesus and Mary in the Coran**, he is basically saying the Coran is ok in this n.252 and we have evidence of this as on Jan. 19 the pope spoke to immigrants, this is by Francis own lips:

"The faith that your parents instilled in you will help you move forward," the pope told the immigrants Jan. 19 at the Basilica of the Sacred Heart of Jesus near Rome's central train station, "you who are Christian, with the Bible, and you who are Muslim, with the Quran."

What about when the pope said that we can't be obsessed by abortion, contraception, and homosexuality, even though he blasted abortion the next day showing hypocrisy due to what he wrote in his exhortation in n.214:

It is not "progressive" to try to resolve problems by eliminating a human life. **On the other hand, it is also true that we have done little to adequately accompany women in very difficult situations, where abortion appears as a quick solution to their profound anguish, especially when the life developing within them is the result of rape or a situation of extreme poverty. Who can remain unmoved before such painful situations?**

Are we picking and choosing what truth to defend? I love the Rosary Michael and I know that you do too, what about when he said:

"I share with you two concerns. One is the Pelagian current that there is in the Church at this moment. There are some restorationist groups. I know some, it fell upon me to receive them in Buenos Aires. And one feels as if one goes back 60 years! Before the

Council... One feels in 1940... An anecdote, just to illustrate this, it is not to laugh at it, I took it with respect, but it concerns me; when I was elected, I received a letter from one of these groups, and they said: "Your Holiness, we offer you this spiritual treasure: 3,525 rosaries." Why don't they say, 'we pray for you, we ask...', but this thing of counting... And these groups return to practices and to disciplines that I lived through - not you, because you are not old - to disciplines, to things that in that moment took place, but not now, they do not exist today..."

(http://rorate-caeli.blogspot.com/2013/06/pope-to-latin-american-religious-full.html)

Now you can see that Francis is no fan of tradition as he says so in the Evangelii Gaudium n.83 and how he attacks priests who denies communion to Catholics who are compromised in their wickedness (read n. 47), But no vortexes were made about this evil.

If you ask who am I, I'm a nobody, I used to be a premium subscriber for more than a year or so (my nick was dysmas), I had to cancel my subscription because I don't like the agenda of picking selectively what truth to defend and what ambiguity to fight, I'm not a sedevacantist... I'm a child of the Novus ordo who found Jesus there, who started to love the Latin mass all thanks to you Michael and the thirst for Jesus...

I have something that I want to live my life by: There's no Mercy without Justice, and Love without truth.

The truth is not a piece out of the whole pie that you can take, the truth is one and you can't pick and choose like many evil priests who are embracing catechism 2358, overlooking 2357, 2359. Didn't Jesus said lots of Mercy in the word of the mount but He followed that saying that salt which no longer has flavor is thrown out? What about the woman who was to be stoned, didn't Jesus showed Mercy, but also told her not to sin again? Truth is one and whole and is worth defending, hopefully you and I can give our lives for it.

Please Michael the only thing I'm saying here is, you need to show courage for everything and anything, St. Athanasius didn't lose heart and today is a saint even though he was excommunicated by the Arian pope, now logic says to us that St. Athanasius is in heaven and we hope that the Arian pope repented in time. Again I'm not a sedevacantist or protestant, in the book I wrote last year (the treasure of the heavens: the biggest robbery in history) part of my dedication was for you my brother, and God knows how I feel about you and that's good enough for me, as all I want for you, me and the whole world is Jesus Mercy, Jesus who loves justice and hates iniquity as describe in psalm 45.

A big hug in Jesus Christ and may He show you tons of Mercy and the way to the Golgotha. Amen

Dr. Rafael Gonzalez

Author of the Treasure of the heavens: the biggest robbery in history, the art of war and diamonds book.

yucanation.blogspot.com

Testimony:

I was at the Church and I needed confession for me and my wife to get married, I went to my priest at the Transfiguration Catholic Church, started my confession and maybe 3 minutes telling him my transgressions, he was preparing to give me absolution.

'Father don't you want to hear my other sins?'

Wal: 'Not necessary, God forgives you.'

I went out with sadness as I had so many sins, but trusted the Lord and as I was doing my penance, God show me my sins in rolls and each one burned in Holy fire in front of my eyes, I was so relieved!

I told my priest about it, he show me a smile and waved goodbye.

The sin of pride

Someone who I love, was praying the Rosary and suddenly saw the evangelicals and Catholics fighting amongst each other, but then they stopped once the rosary was handed to both of them and both started to recite the Rosary walking towards the Golgotha to be crucified with our Lord.

For "everyone who calls on the name of the Lord will be saved." Romans 10:13

When Jesus came into the World and despite being the owner of infinite Glory He became poor, shepherds and Wiseman Kings (pagans) came before Him and in harmony (as ONE) they worship and adore, that was in His 1st coming, but now, for His 2nd coming will He find the same harmony? Will He find the Evangelicals in union with the Messianic Jews, Catholics, Coptic, Orthodox like He and His Almighty Father are, one? One in love and truth...

Before any further you need to know this, without any arrogance or sentiment of pride, I say this with respect and humility, The Catholic Church was establish by Jesus Christ Himself.

The same Catholic Church who is falling more day by day in a deep apostasy...

All of us who try to be Christians we need to put down our guns, before there was any orthodox and Coptic churches, existed only the Catholic Church which had many Saints and many Judas in their ranks...

Whatever happened in the past it happened because many Judas had their way in both sides, but we need to embrace His commands in order to please our Lord...

Jesus said to them, "Very truly I tell you, unless you eat the flesh of the Son of Man and drink his blood, you have no life in you." John 6:53

Without the Sacraments we are lost and we ALL need the Eucharist to be raised in the last day...

Whoever eats my flesh and drinks my blood has eternal life, and I will raise them up at the last day. John 6:54

I remember a dear friend of mine who is an Evangelical, she knows that Jesus IS in the Holy Eucharist, she knows it is the Body of our Lord, but she respects His commands and wouldn't dare to eat His flesh without permission from the Catholic Church; she was suffering because she liked being an Evangelical while craving for the infinite love in

His Holy Flesh. Somebody told her the experience St. Therese Lissieux had with her first communion:

"It was like a drop of water reuniting for the first time with the ocean" St Therese Lissieux

So my friend went to a Catholic priest and now she is sacrificing herself for the love of God, to unite her with Jesus, to be that drop of water, her sacrifice will not go unnoticed in heaven.

Pride can take life away from you, the same pride which is turning most of us Catholics into the new Pharisees, humility will only please our Lord let's seek to be little, let's seek to serve, let's seek to fulfilled His commands.

When Pharisees reign when Jesus was born, they all thought they were superior... nowadays some people think they are already saved and relax themselves, even though spiritual war is all over, Evangelicals thinking "once saved always saved" Catholics "Outside of the Catholic Church there's no salvation" That phrase right there made believe most Catholics that they are all saved and they have the RIGHT to condemn to hell non-Catholics.

Those who condemn others to hell are condemning themselves by not letting Jesus be the Judge, let's humble ourselves, let's please Him in the most perfect way, let's imitate Him... He says "Learn from Me for I am meek and humble of Heart." Mat 11:29

He didn't say "proud", He said "humble"... so let's practice that now, every word in the bible has the Holy Spirit imprinted... so let's repeat a few words from the bible itself and we will end with a petition... pray with me all you Christians out there disregarding religion:

"Hail Mary, full of grace, the Lord is with thee... Blessed are thou among women and blessed is the fruit of thy womb... Jesus"

Petition: "Holy Mary, Mother of God (Jesus) pray for us sinners now and at the hour of our death. Amen"

Now let's seek to be humble in imitation of Jesus who pleased the Father, so let's please Him by following His commands... Let's strive to have the sacraments the RIGHT way, through THE Church that He started, the Church that will not end despite starting tribulation and embracing Apostasy, let's not condemn to hell anyone, because that's God's job.

We are almost at the start of the revealing of the Antichrist, and the Eucharist WILL BE CANCELED SOON fulfilling the prophecies of Prophet Daniel 12:11, Mary of Magdalene (John 20:13) and Jesus (Mat 24:15). Terror is slowly creeping in and once full blown apostasy sets in, it'll be difficult having the sacraments in those days and you NEED to have life within you, **so cast away pride**, the weapon of choice by Heaven will be perseverance through the Rosary... Full Apostasy is almost upon us, throw pride away and suffer tribulation with us united in harmony and on our way to be crucified with our Lord. Amen

"LEARN from Me for I am meek and humble of heart."

Judging error is evil?

"Stop judging, that you may not be judged." (Mat 7:1)

This part of Matthew means don't be a hypocrite.

Why we are saying this? Because of John 7:24, it says: "Stop judging by appearances, but judge justly."

It is clear that God is the Just Judge and He is the one who needs to Judge and condemn because of our sins, not us. One day St Francis of Assisi told his friars who were about to go out and evangelize thieves, he told them: "Do not tell them 'do not steal' because they won't listen, instead be an example."

Is he saying that it's wrong to tell them how wrong their actions were? NO!!

Again: "Stop judging by appearances, but judge justly." " (John 7:24).

Report doctrinal error is an essential part of the ministry of any genuine preacher and must be done for the people of God. So when we see necessary to criticize the tactics and teachings of others, must be done using the Word of God as the standard y not our own ideas.

(http://www.cuttingedge.org/sp/p187.htm)

Then scandals will be multiplied, our Order divided, and many others will be completely destroyed, because the error will be accepted instead of opposing it. (Prophecy of St. Francis of Assisi)

Again:

Because ERROR will be accepted instead of opposing it.

Being a hypocrite, is not seeing truth in one self, if we are truth less we are blind and can lead to error. The truth is Jesus!

S. Francis of Assisi said: Oppose error! There are many out there accepting error.

No one was more obedient than St Francis of Assisi and yet he talks about objecting to error... Of the one coming dressed as a sheep while being a wolf!!!

Some say we must obey regardless of error... NO! We must obey although there's a false prophet on top... NO! For the love of whom don't know error, we can't shut our mouths!!!

Poor me if I don't speak truth!!!

Fatima: Spoke about apostasy in the Church! By obedience we have to ignore error? John spoke of a soon to come apostasy in revelations and we have to keep quiet? NO!!!!

At the time of tribulation there's a man, not canonically elected, will rise to the pontificate, and his cunning endeavor shall lead many to error and death. (Prophecy of St. Francis of Assisi)

Attacking ERROR is Christian... the world always comes up with excuses that one judges, but in Ephesians 5:11 says:

"Take no part in the fruitless works of darkness; rather expose them,"

Why the Blessed Virgin has constantly appeared? Because there are many priests not exposing error taking souls to hell!

Atheists go to heaven? We must obey our conscience? We are all redeemed?

When a prophet speaks on behalf of God speaks the truth and the truth is indivisible... When a false prophet speaks changes truth... So he doesn't speak from God but from and for the world.

He'll be consistent changing the truth and many will cheer, instead of denouncing error... that's from the enemy! Many miracles will happen, for me the only miracle is the Eucharist...

They will change the meaning of the Eucharist or abolish the Sacrament if so, Dan 12:11 will be fulfilled and the abomination of desolation will be established; DON'T GO AWAY FROM THE CATHOLIC CHURCH, AND DON'T ACCEPT ERROR.

May God bless you through Jesus Christ. Amen.

SHALOM (Pray for Israel)

For you are a people holy to the LORD *your God. The* LORD *your God has chosen you out of all the peoples on the face of the earth to be his people, his treasured possession.* Deut 7: 6

But you are a chosen people, a royal priesthood, a holy nation, God's special possession, that you may declare the praises of him who called you out of darkness into his wonderful light. 1 Peter 2: 9

God has never gone against his Holy Word, there is NO doubt... Israel IS the chosen people of God, they were the recipient of the first covenant and although the Jews broke it according to the Holy Word of Yahweh, the Father Almighty in Jeremiah, but despite His Chosen People have broken the old covenant, God shows infinite Mercy to His people and let them know His plan of love:

"The days are coming," declares the LORD, "when I will make a new covenant with the people of Israel and with the people of Judah. It will not be like the covenant I made with their ancestors when I took them by the hand to lead them out of Egypt, because they broke my covenant, though I was a husband to them," declares the LORD. "This is the covenant I will make with the people of Israel after that time," declares the LORD. "I will put my law in their minds and write it on their hearts. I will be their

God, and they will be my people. No longer will they teach their neighbor, or say to one another, 'Know the LORD,' because they will all know me, from the least of them to the greatest," declares the LORD. "For I will forgive their wickedness and will remember their sins no more." Jer 31: 31-34

Although, when that promise of God came, the new covenant in Jesus Christ and was rejected by the ecclesiastical hierarchy of that time, yet Israel continues to be the Chosen People of God despite their broken covenant.

Therefore it is the duty of every Catholic in their daily prayers for the people of Israel, that God gives the necessary graces and blessings they need to accept Jesus as their Lord and Savior, we must never lodge hatred in our hearts, rather pray for all who rejects Jesus around the world for its salvation and especially for Israel.

Our Blessed Mother Mary in Fatima asked us to pray for all sinners for their conversion, Jesus asks us to pray for our enemies and those who persecute us; imagine the joy they'll have when they see us that we pray for the conversion of the people where they were born and suffered.

Therefore, whosoever does NOT pray for Israel for their conversion, in other words, prays for them to accept Jesus into their hearts, is not Catholic.

Just as when Jesus was born, the Jewish shepherds and the wise men came together to worship Him, the same will happen in the end when we finally get together as brothers to worship and receive our King in His 2nd coming.

Pray for Israel and its conversion... THERE IS NOTHING MORE CATHOLIC, TO PRAY FOR THE CONVERSION OF MEN AND EVEN MORE IF IT IS FOR ISRAEL.

SHALOM.

Dear priests, hear me...

Servants of God, dear priests, pastors... those who swore to take the cup of suffering, please hear me...

Today only few in the Church see what's going on, we see many coming out from the seminaries believing that they have a career in their hands, a career... not a walk, a path right on the streets of Jerusalem, with a cross in their backs with their flesh tore open like our Lord did.

It seems that the desire to become martyrs have ceased.

Today, 'Mercy' is been called as the end of certain language that could offend certain people, called as to give the Eucharist to the unrepentant... and those who call themselves "servants of God", His disciples, who ARE supposed to know their Master better, are betraying Him.

It seems that contrary to what happened when Jesus was alive, when 11 disciples and 1 traitor walked with Him, today feels like it is 11 traitors and 1 disciple everywhere, Isaiah has been fulfilled...

"Woe to those who call evil good and good evil, who put darkness for light and light for darkness, who put bitter for sweet and sweet for bitter... Therefore, as tongues of fire lick up straw and as dry grass sinks down in the flames, so their roots will decay and their flowers blow away like dust; FOR THEY HAVE REJECTED THE LAW of the LORD ALMIGHTY and spurned the word of the Holy One of Israel." Isaiah 5:20, 24.

The World has embraced apostasy everywhere and we look to our pastors and they either spread poison or stay silent... is rare to find a priest who holds dear what our Lord taught.

Some, point fingers to Vatican II, and yes Vatican II happened (unfortunately), despite heaven's advice in Fatima, it happened... but Vatican II is long gone and Vatican II is not a man, it doesn't have a soul, a soul that could go to hell, but you and I can.

It feels like NO PRIEST has the desire to become a Martyr... silence is seen and the pulpits filled with empty words about the current situation, everyone is afraid and souls are in jeopardy.

I'm afraid for my 3 children, I'm afraid that they are raised in a culture that you could get penalized by reading the Gospel alone, as the Gospel has words that can offend most.

The enemies of Christ have infiltrated the Church in so many levels, that we only think of what out Blessed Lady said in La Salette:

"Rome will lose the faith and becomes the seat of the antichrist"

Rome, the eternal city, where the seat of Peter is, where most of the confusion is flowing from, is confusion from God? Does Rome have the power to contradict our Lord and call it Mercy? Vatican II happened and FEW DID something... Today? Nothing just more confusion...

No one wants to call the sword a sword, no one wants to call error a heresy, no one wants to save souls, it seems that too much is at stake, that you could lose your career...

Career... Is that what it is? The desire to Love our Lord in ALL His commandments is NOT a career... but IN YOUR FACE suffering, all for the salvation of souls.

Martyrdom, the cup of suffering taken by most of you, have been denied by your omissions, words and deeds, the Laity is on fire and you dare to seat and do nothing... This is why our Lord sweat dropped like blood in the ground.

BELIEVE AGAIN, pursuit salvation for all of us, this are dark times, but those on top have called a beautiful and bright times instead, confusion... that's the name of the game the devil is playing and most who are supposed to be God's servants are playing with so much enthusiasm.

The Cheering of the World is their gain, while the souls are falling in the Abyss, but most don't believe in Hell anymore... RECLAIM THE CUP OF SUFFERING, RECLAIM THE DESIRE TO SUFFER FOR CHRIST, HAVE THE DESIRE OF MARTYRDOM, and souls shall be save from confusion...

ARE YOU AFRAID? So am I... it is my hope that you are afraid to reject our Lord's desires in His commandments, not that you are afraid for your career. Vatican II passed by, it is gone and the main object back then of that council was to relax souls rejecting Phil 2:12...

"...continue to work out your salvation with fear and trembling,.."
Vatican II succeeded but has passed, today we have Bishops proclaiming straight up wickedness as 'Mercy', are you willing to let our souls to fall in the mud? Will you let iniquity to be taught from the

pulpits out of obedience? This Synod is here today echoing Vatican II in the worst way: apostasy.

OBEY GOD FIRST and seek His Kingdom, lead us to heaven through your desire to please Him, embrace Martyrdom, embrace the cup you have forgotten you took, save us in His Name. Amen

Blessings

Traditionalist wannabe beliefs.

(My beliefs)

1) I believe that all life comes from the hands of God, from the smallest to the biggest, and His creation, us... are in charge, to use what He has given us, only to Honor Him. (Gen 1,2)

* Most people abuse the resources given for monetary gain and many in the world are dying, not even what it falls from their tables is given, if a profit isn't attached (Luke 16:21).

* Evolution was planned to dishonor God as it is an atheist way to throw away His Love and Mercy.

* When a servant of God throws away one part of the word of God, because it's not logical (contraception, abortion, evolution, etc...), or it's not in line with science, or because is what the sheep of today loves - the world's Kool aid -, WE NEED TO PRAY FOR THEIR CONVERSION.

* Life came from God's hands SO abortion is murder.

2) I believe that there was a serious and malicious intent to teach indirectly (through local catechism) and directly (Cardinals, Bishops, priests) that the tridentine mass was no more, Benedict XVI clarified and squash this intent with his motu propio, thanks be to God for Benedict XVI His true Vicar.

3) I believe that Mercy is breathed each day like air, Mercy that let us live our lives (Mat 4:45) and Mercy that knocks at our door for us to truly live (Rev 3:20).

* The most greatest sign today that God's Mercy is still raining on all earth, is that humanity is still receiving new descendants each day, Mothers all around are crying tears of love seeing their babies for the first time, despite God's hands hurting so much because of the evilness and cold hearts on earth, God's Mercy is still all around us.

4) I believe, the Eucharist is the very flesh of God and without it there is a LIMIT on how far spirituality in a soul could go... True and sincere repentance, willingness to stop sinning, the pursuit of being pure, surrendering our own will, is the door to a true communion with God while eating and swallowing the very Flesh God.

5) I believe, the 2nd most used and misunderstood Catholic quote is "outside of the Church there's no salvation", this quote by St Cyprian is 100% true, but it's most used to point fingers and condemned people to hell, with those people who are not Catholics... there are Christians living the Gospel with more love than Catholics. The Christians, Coptic, Messianic Jews getting martyred in the Middle East today and because some traditionalist says so they are in hell? NO... the correct interpretation is "outside of the Church there's no salvation...because outside of the Church there's only the world".

Who are of the World? Those who despite knowing the truth sells the gospel for 30 coins, liberalism priests, laity, atheists, Muslims, Buddhists, some other strange religions and Freemasons. Did you know that more than 50% of the Catholic population accepts homosexuality, contraception, and abortion as a "right" and a "way of life" that is acceptable by God and when presented with the Holy word of God only 1% or less changes their lives? And out of that 1% that change at that time goes back to their old believes? BUT there are Muslims, Evangelicals and others who hasn't received a good proclamation of the Gospel and the truth in the Sacraments, and this people give honor to Almighty Father in their own way more than most Catholics...so the moral is: DON'T JUDGE the person, judge the acts!

* Those who condemn people to hell condemn themselves. (Mat 7:11)

* Again: We need to Judge ACTS, not people. (1 Cor 2:15)

6) I believe in the Catholic Church which is the one true faith, the Bride of Christ and it is within the Sacraments that souls thirsty of Jesus, can achieve more spiritual gain; other Christian religions benefit of the Bride of Christ as those who die in such religions will be judged by God according to their deeds (Mar 9:39), but nevertheless the sound doctrine, the one of the Catholic Church should be preach to all corners of the world, for the sake of souls to achieve spiritual perfection.

7) I believe that Mercy alone cannot be, as Mercy and Justice comes from the same source: Love, if we preach Mercy we need to ask for true repentance, sincere restitution and sacrifice... Justice can be seen in one side for some but as soon Justice is given, Mercy is receive by others, and the reverse is true (John 8:11).

8) I believe communion in the hand is a sin... not recognizing who stands in front of us when the time comes; whoever receives communion in the hand, get their spirituality set backwards.

9) I believe the Novus Ordo was permitted by God for a reason and that reason can be seen by the spiritual eye clearly, there is a whole crucifixion process going on in every Novus ordo until the sacrifice is finally at hand to be offered to Almighty Father, and this is what will separate those who truly love Him and those who truly don't.

* The Bread is still becoming the Flesh of God by transubstantiation, but the process has become the same that happened 2000 years ago, only a few did suffered with Jesus all the way to the death Hill and this is also true today, in the Novus Ordo: the spats, scourging, mockery and violence is still going on.

* The Novus Ordo will serve as the base for the abomination of desolation sadly, as APOSTASY can and will be more easily set than in the mass that every saint embraced, the Latin Mass.

10) I believe that, the Divine Mercy Chaplet and the Sacred hearts of Jesus and Mary were given to a wounded Church and delayed the rampant ascend of the anti-church backed by the secret sect and the secular world, Jesus had to allow the Divine Mercy Chaplet to be questioned and objected until a bishop of Poland discovered the mistakes made by the CDF and in 1978 those objections were cleared and the truth won and the devotion was accepted, weeks after the fact, that very same Bishop became pope and St John Paul II.

11) I believe that Jesus has presented His will through Holy servants, priests, seers and prophets who like Him are ridiculed, mocked and silenced to the day... Jesus out of Love, He has sent them, in Fatima, Akita, Quito, La Salette, Garabandal, Colombia, Lourdes and Ireland... and He did this to warn us of His Mercy, Justice and fulfillment of His Word, but like Father Pio, St John of the Cross, St Benedict and many more, they were rejected, imprisoned and even plotted to kill them...

12) I believe that Mercy is in play for me to see, how easy is to switch from apostles to traitors if we don't embrace His Holy Word with Joy and a thankful heart (Mat 19:14)...

May the Lord let us wake up in time to meet the groom, as it right now a voice is calling: "the groom is coming" (Mat 25:6)

--------- o ---------

"I Believe that Jesus Loves me, I believe that I am His property, I believe in Almighty Father who gave me His only Son, I believe in the Holy Spirit, I believe in my Blessed Mother Mary who will pray for my salvation, I believe in the 2000 tradition taught in the one true faith: the Catholic Church, I believe that if I abandon myself into the ocean of Jesus infinite Mercy with my true repentance and will for holiness, I can be what He envisioned of me when He created me... a part of His family." Amen.

Truth or obedience, which one came first.

Which came first Truth or obedience? Nowadays there is a very hard persecution inside the church to whatever feels, sounds and looks orthodox or better said: tradition, the apostles rely on tradition because many were deceive by the false prophets...

"See to it that no one captivate you with an empty, seductive philosophy according to human tradition, according to the elemental powers of the world and not according to Christ." Col 2:8

After Vatican II many fell in the false notion that everything that was tradition belong in the past, as new ways about administering the Catholic Church was to be done and leave the old ways in the past totally disregarding what the apostles once said:

"Therefore, brothers, stand firm and hold fast to the traditions that you were taught, either by an oral statement or by a letter of ours." Thes 2:15

Tradition was and still under attack, many bishops didn't want the Latin mass anymore as it was something that most needed to get rid of, when the

SSPX was took by Marcel Lefebvre, he saw a real danger of all apostolic tradition to be forgotten for good, this is why today there's a feud between the new way and the old way.

I have spent my whole life in the Novus ordo mass and the catechism they taught us when we were kids, never mentioned that there was a mass in Latin, a mass which gave birth to all of the church's saints, it was until I was 41 years old that I went to a Latin mass, did not understood one single word but, yet it was supernatural and very holy, in two words to describe it: *heaven's mass*.

Now don't get ahead of ourselves both masses are allowed, both masses are legal, it's just that one has a sacrifice and the other has a sacrifice with the whole process of the crucifixion as well, in other words in the new mass we let our Lord to suffer the same process He once did, people spitting, saying names to Him, mockery and finally the crucifixion like 2000 years ago.

The SSPX that Lefebvre took evolution as the life raft of the Church, the SSPX felt at the time that tradition was been sacrificed in order to please the world, this insistence of modernism in the Church dates back since Judas betrayed Jesus, as you can see Judas, took sides with the world even though he had seen the sick been cured, demons thrown to hell and many more miracles...

Apostle Paul insists to stay within the apostolic teachings taught by them in order to avoid false doctrines and apostates. I'm not a part of the SSPX but many had called me lefebrist, protestant, Antichrist and false prophet... many in my dear Catholic Church call anybody lefebrist, traditionalist or legalist with pure rejection and smirks of hate going against all the teachings left by Jesus Himself, many are proud to be a lefebrist, but we need to be humble and happy to be just a Catholic.

Truth is within Jesus, but we prefer obedience even though whoever in higher power above us is totally wrong (example. Francis: "The old pact of the Jews it's still good.", "Proselytism is a solemn nonsense" or Card. Reinhardt Marx: "Hell doesn't exist.").

Thinking because someone wants to actually follow Jesus instead of a man is some sort of a scandal, think of St. Athanasius for a moment... he was excommunicated by the Arian Pope and most of the Catholic Church DID push apostasy on many souls went to hell... but St. Athanasius followed the truth, not obedience... in the end Jesus Mercy won and the Church was saved from **ERROR!**

Are we saying go to the SSPX, of course not! If you go to them is totally on you and we have to say it is totally safe because they ARE Catholic; if they weren't they wouldn't have sat down with Benedict and the excommunications uplifted, they're **NOT** sedevacantists as they do recognize the pope as the head of the Church, that's why they went to Benedict XVI, but what they won't recognize is Vatican II, even our Lady in Fatima said that an **EVIL** council was to be done.

Don't ever call anybody a lefebrist because we are all Catholic trying to get our celestial home, if someone says that the SSPX is not Catholic, walk away... you don't want to be participant of their sin, again, I'm a Novus ordo guy who happens to like tradition and I don't have an SSPX in St. Petersburg FL (Google it), even my own family doesn't want to go to Diocesan Latin Mass... but we need to recognize what our Lord likes and doesn't likes, we need to seek to be more spiritual.

May Jesus gives tons of His Sweet Mercy and shows you the way to Golgotha. Amen.

Prayer: Tears of the Novus Ordo.

(Please pray)

Oh my Lord Jesus, I found Thee in the Novus
Ordo...
Oh my Lord Jesus, forgive me all the times I took
Your Holy Body in my hands...
Oh my Lord forgive the times I stood thinking it was
very uncomfortable to kneel...

Jesus, my God, my Savior and my guide...
Please forgive the times when I profane Holy
ground with a haughtiness attitude...
Oh my Lord Jesus, forgive the times when I thought
I was doing something good in front of You, but in
reality it was something
Very mundane, forgive me for not thinking of You,
my beautiful and faithful Lord!

Forgive the times I went to the altar to receive
communion without having confession priory
Without love and without expectations...
Forgive the times thinking that because I was
young, You understood my poor form of praise and
worship, when in fact, deep down I was giving You
my leftovers...

You saved me every second of my existence and went to the mass to feast my eyes... not to find You...

I found Thee in the Novus Ordo and I cried with happiness when I did,
I also cry in sadness to see how little spiritual I was in the past...
Lord, let me embrace your Mercy, let me serve You with love, take your hand and lead me to the Golgotha so I could be crucified
Beside You, let me die of love for You... and let me see only Thee...
Let me be more spiritual Jesus, help me to devote myself to your Mother Mary,
Let me reach heaven, so I can adore perfectly your Father, You and the Holy Spirit...

In the Novus ordo I found You, and in greenest pastures You will take me in the Latin Mass...
How Lovely You are Jesus... Amen.

Testimony

My family and I were in Church and I wasn't going to take the Eucharist due to my many sins, when the time came up the only one who stood up to get the Eucharist was my youngest boy Axel, he came and said:

- "Let's go dad, come with me."

I replied: 'My son, you should go alone, because I haven't went to confession yet, but you should run to Him (Jesus), like He is the only thing in the world you need, go and take Him.'

Well he went, I started to think about other things, my financial problems, the house, etc... when this taste came into my mouth, the taste of bread, I was intensifying more and more until at the end of mass this Eucharist fell down my throat.

I was so happy, Jesus pardoned my sins and gave a miracle that I wasn't expecting, I wasn't worthy but He made me worthy.

When I told my priest I said it was a friend whom a love so much, since I am my own friend and I love myself I wasn't saying a lie; I had to say it like that because many were watching me in my church as a freak, or exhibitionist since I always kneeled and took the Eucharist in the tongue.

But Blessed be God forever because of His Love for me, an unworthy worm.

Open Letter to Christopher Ferrara...

My dear lawyer, blessings upon blessings for you and your family, may Christ continue to give you clarity in this dark times.

Dear friend, I write to you this words with the hope that somehow you read them, I don't earn anything but rejection and persecution outside and inside my house, whenever I sat down in front of my computer to write anything that is related to the Church and how people have forgotten about He who hangs nailed to the Cross.

I remember one of those days when you sat down with another excellent Catholic, Michael Matt and reflected about the situation of the Church with 'pope' Francis, I remember how both of you were talking back and forth and nibble about how, while in Argentina, he let the 'curas villeros' to commit sacrilege by giving the Eucharist to irregular couples.

Everybody saw how Francis while in Argentina, fought against this so called homosexual 'matrimony' (because he didn't want it to be called a matrimony), everyone saw the outside and cheered, but when Bergoglio met with a group of Bishops and told them that it was best to recognize gay marriage as 'civil unions', all were shocked.

Gay activists reach out to him and his excuse about his proselytism against gay marriage was, that he was 'persecuted' by conservatives, but he respects them and wanted for gay couples to be recognize as an 'union', not as a marriage.

He got elected with the sensational help of a group of progressives who proselytize for him to get elected and this was reported by Iverigh and in Card. Danneels autobiography.

When he said that he was reprimanded because he didn't talked much about abortion, contraception and homosexuality gives a hint, on how conservatives were on his case back in Argentina.

Now, is it a surprise that he called an Argentinian woman, who is married to a divorced man and how he told her to switch to another Parrish to get the Eucharist? Is it a surprise that the wicked relatio in 2014 was made with his approval? Tell me if it was when a transsexual's feet was washed by him and how this person received the Eucharist?

Is it a surprise that people nowadays in the Vatican receives the Eucharist in the hand? Or how this instrumentum laboris stood out there for a year running around the world without any rejection by Francis? Is it a surprise that when Germany proclaimed that they were not a branch of the Vatican they weren't called schismatics, but when Poland rejected the synod and chose to resist, Francis in his final homily addressed the 'cloud' of schism in central Europe?

No, no surprises at all...

We knew what was going to happen, it is prophesied that the continual sacrifice shall be taken away (Daniel 12:11) as those who are supposed to know the Master and Teacher better, are so enthusiastic to give what's holy to the dogs (Mat 7:6)

No surprises with Francis, he says it all with his deeds. Everything he does is with ambiguity... nothing straight.

The instrumentum laboris shows heresies in just a few paragraphs, heresies buried with tons of other beautiful paragraphs, the same happened with the final relatio, which was favored by vote.

The family is now weakened and those who chose to live as sister and brother, their efforts, were thrown to the mud, yet... no surprises.

Why I'm I writing this words to you, I want you to be more courageous than you have been, I want everyone to be courageous and see what is going on: "Rome has lost the faith..."

Resisting, is the duty of all faithful Catholics, by NOT staying quiet, by telling the Catholic world the full truth, that this man HAS preached modernism before and after seating in the throne of Peter, and if modernism is the heresy of all heresies, then no pope can be a heretic and at the same time pope.

BY Catholic law, we shouldn't follow wolves in sheep clothing and that's the truth, even more when they so happily show their wolfy face to the public...

There is a true pope, whether he wants it or not, a pope who defrocked 600 pedophile priests, a pope who revealed the truth of the Muslims, that proclaimed that nostra actate as 'dangerous', lifted the excommunications, and gave a motu propio in favor of the Latin mass.

Pope Benedict is the true pope and like Peter, who was taken where he didn't want to go (John 21:18), Benedict XVI has been martyred (in the dry sense), but heaven is behind him...

Francis has been permitted by heaven to murky the waters, to chastise the Catholic Church for rejecting the path of tradition, which was foretold in Fatima.

Francis is indeed an antipope and with his many deeds, past and present reflects who he truly is, and what about the future? I'll finish that sentence form La Salette above: "... and becomes the seat of the antichrist"

Mr. Ferrara, it is time to be brave and remain faithful, it is time to call the sword a sword like you and many have, BUT it is also time to call the wolf as he is, so I pray for you and all to be brave.

Jesus has called us to be wise as the serpent and innocent as doves when we are amongst wolves (Mat 10:16), and this is the best description on how you guys have conducted your behavior until now, but many who don't know the faith are embracing what he call himself as 'teachings', which, in summary... the words: true repentance, abomination and sin are not a part of his vocabulary, this is how false teachers talk.

For Francis everything is beautiful and fantastic until is time to hold God's law in place and give mercy to traditionalists, this is another evidence, by the teachings of our forefathers... how antipopes behave, by slandering those who are faithful with bad words (hermeneutical, rosary counter, museum of mummies, closed minded, etc...)

Please, defend the truth all the way, that's all I wanted to say, the truth all the way...

When all the disciples were running away in pain and in fear, John embraced our Blessed Mother and never let go, he stood with Her in front of Her Son and despite the Horror, they stood by the truth all the way.

We all have a choice... to stand by the truth all the way to the Golgotha or to reject it like Judas did... Woe to those who prefer the easy way out...

Not all who goes to the Golgotha are martyred the same way, the other disciples who ran in fear eventually took the chalice and all got martyred in different ways, so blessed are those who suffers in the name of Christ by standing with the truth all the way.

Thanks for reading my dear Lawyer, a big hug in Jesus Christ. Amen

To the Remnant newspaper:

On the video "Why pope Francis is the Idol of secular media" the Remnant acknowledges between minutes 15:50 and 16:10 that pope Francis wanted to transform the Papacy into "Buenos Aires" where he allowed the Eucharist to be given away to many irregular couples....

Many have reported about this sacrilege, it is a certainty, this happened back in Buenos Aires, and we are not talking about when he allowed a belly for hire child from a transvestite and his couple to be baptized in a Catholic Temple, or manifesting in favor for homosexual civil unions to a gathering of Bishops... no, nothing compared to that, giving the Eucharist, the Holy flesh of God to the unrepentant, people in irregular marital situations knowing beforehand and not caring that's beyond bad. It seems that in the mind of many liberal priests and Bishops, as long "mercy" is provided, God would understand right? Like He could contradict Himself by "allowing" such a thing, thinking that God can give you a "break" and ignore His Holy Word...

"For anyone who eats and drinks without discerning the body, eats and drinks judgment on himself." 1 Cor 11:29

How about priests who don't care about the sinfulness of those who don't want to repent and worse, when those on top allows it and make it sure is alright...

47. The Church is called to be the house of the Father, with doors always wide open. One concrete sign of such openness is that our church doors should always be open, so that if someone, moved by the Spirit, comes there looking for God, he or she will not find a closed door. There are other doors that should not be closed either. Everyone can share in some way in the life of the Church; everyone can be part of the community, <u>nor should the doors of the sacraments be closed for simply any reason.</u> This is especially true of the sacrament which is itself "the door": baptism. The Eucharist, although it is the fullness of sacramental life, is not a prize for the perfect but a powerful medicine and nourishment for the weak. These convictions have pastoral consequences that we are called to consider with prudence and boldness. Frequently, we act as arbiters of grace rather than its facilitators. But the Church is not a toll house; it is the house of the Father, where there is a place for everyone, with all their problems. (Evangelii Gaudiim #47)

Please define Sacrilege my brethren... you like to shout to the heavens how seriously wrong this papacy is doing things, which is true, Francis has being like this since always; Sacrilege... which is more than heresy, more than apostasy itself, Sacrilege by someone who knows (Mario Bergoglio, Francis), is more grave than someone who don't know the faith, but Judas knew and didn't care.

Catholic Law says that a heretic cannot become pope even with the majority of the votes, yet the remnant newspaper likes to flash laws in all their videos and articles and ignore what Jesus said, that we shouldn't follow false prophets... priests being allowed to give the Eucharist in a such irresponsible way and the Remnant acknowledging that this actually happened and then say: "yeah he is a validly elected pope", we need to ask ourselves: do they know something we don't? About how sacrilege operates and is?

I don't doubt people being happy about the confusion overflowing by Francis and how faithful priests stay silent while the flock falls away, I don't doubt the Remnant's compromise to the truth, but like some, who defends the truth up to certain extend, we need to tell you, truth needs to be defended all the way, in its fullness not just a large part, the entire truth.

A heretic cannot be pope, so Francis is not pope, by his many transgressions, his gigantic and horrible Sacrilege which is solidified by that #47 exhortation. The actions of those who he appointed, those who have given the Eucharist to wicked people (Wuerl, Cuppich...) has given lights in whom he really is, a false prophet.

True, it is too easy to say "he is not pope", yes it's easy to say he is a false prophet, yes it's easy to judge, yes it's easy to point out the wood in our brothers eyes and not see our own, and sedevacantism has been a sin and will always been a sin, but telling the truth is not a sin... we are not sedevacantist, I have love every pope I had since childhood, and all were valid despite a flawed council... but calling people sedevacantists, because they consider pope Francis not a true pope but an antipope, a Judas, a false prophet, because they have seen the truth in the light of this sacrilege and many more evidences that puts question marks on the validity of this papacy, is irresponsible and you need to apologize.

Resisting this pope and denouncing the demolition, denouncing the lies is the right thing to do, our rosaries, sacrifice, and our NO to the false Mercy preach from the top is a must...

Our Lady of La Salette said it, "Rome will lose the faith and becomes the seat of the Antichrist" and I'm not saying he is the Antichrist, but he's sure helping him.

God bless Archbishop Lefebvre for his commitment to the truth, God bless pope Benedict for the Light he has shown, God bless Mr. Voris for defending the truth up to an extent... the truth suffers violence and it is not my wish to scorn good people and you are, excellent people, I would give my life for you in an instant... but saying "Yeah the pope gave the Eucharist away in Argentina to irregular couples" and also saying "Francis is valid", while it is Law that NO heretic can become pope, admitting he is guilty of such crime in Argentina and pointing fingers at what you call "sedevacantists" for saying he is FALSE, is a slap on the face.

Maybe I'm wrong... maybe I'm living in a world were giving away the Eucharist to the unrepentant, confirming heretic Bruno Forte, letting Wuerl to handle the next Synod, and letting cardinal Kasper to spread poison is not confirming LIBERALISM, which, is right there sitting at the top.

LIBERALISM and PETER cannot co-exist, just ask St Paul when he rebuked Peter... Francis IS not a true pope because he was a heretic then, he is a heretic now and my proof is everywhere in his bad fruits...

Lastly... LIBERALISM and PETER cannot co-exist, Peter is the rock, not a lot of sand, apologize Remnant and continue your spot on work... I love you in Jesus Christ.

Dr. Rafael Gonzalez

A Neo-catholic who happens to love the Latin mass.

Author of The Treasure of the Heavens: The biggest robbery in history, the art of war and diamonds books.

Tridentine Forever!

The other day someone asked me:

"Do you understand Latin?"

We were at a friend's house, for the blessing of their new house... after the prayers and the blessing, we started to talk about the Latin Mass (among other topics), at the end of the talk, a man participating on those topics asked me that question above, my answer was: "No I don't..."

"Then why you go there?"

"Because (I said), all the Saints of the Catholic Church went to the Latin Mass, that's why..."

The Latin Mass has a supernatural feel, which starts right when I see those feet walking towards the altar, the feet of he who will offer the Sacrifice and proclaim the good news of Jesus Christ.

When the priest elevates the Holy Flesh of Jesus to offer it to Almighty Father, then, like those who grab his cloak, at the same time I feel the entire flock grabbing his cloak too, elevating our prayers, hearts, hopes and our sorrow for all the past wrong forgiven or not...

The chains of sin have no power, on those, who have receive forgiveness due to a sincere and broken heart... Almighty Father receives the perfect sacrifice with pain and Love each time, pain for those who reject Him while eating the Holy Flesh in grave sin and Love for those who have humble themselves before God with sincere unworthiness.

We are ALL unworthy, but a humble and broken heart, God will not reject (psalm 51:17)...

God makes the impossible possible with those who wants to Love Him, love until it HURTS... if you Love the Lord and you are not persecuted, then something is wrong, because the hurt is pure persecution and that's how a true Christian rejoices, when suffering in His Name.

Tridentine Forever! Yes... the persecuted mass, the mass that Saints grew with, not pointing fingers to people, not telling them that they are condemned, but showing the world holiness due to that Love, everlasting Love that will get you so much hurt... so much persecution.

Have you notice something? How much persecution the Tridentine Mass has and almost nothing in the Novus Ordo and Neocatechumenal mass?

But even though... The Eucharist is still becoming the Holy Flesh of Jesus in this masses and IF there's no Latin mass in your area, then you need to eat His Holy Flesh for you to have life truly (John 6:53), so go to this other Masses.

But there's no comparison...

The Tridentine Mass (Latin), is there for you to grow in Spirit but the other Masses have a ceiling due to the mockery, banalities... the whole process of Crucifixion.

I don't understand Latin, but my heart is thrown down to Jesus feet for Him to have Mercy on me, my family, friends, colleagues and nation... Yes Tridentine Forever, there hasn't been a Saint been born after 1965 like Padre Pio or St. Therese of Lissieux, those who are spiritual knows exactly what this means.

May God gives you the thirst to Honor Him more and more, may Jesus lead you to a greener path in the Latin Mass, may He gives you the Honor to Love Him so much until it HURTS. Amen

Last night

Last night I was doing the Rosary when a picture of my Lord came in to my mind, He was severely beaten and swollen, I was in shock as I was about to start the mystery of the taking of the cross by Jesus, I could see the face of my Lord screaming in pain... Started the procession of the cross when the first fall took place, I was suddenly running into the scene, I was shouting: "The King of Glory has fallen, the King of Glory has fallen..." I was watching in distaste how everybody was cursing at Him despite I was shouting those words, how much hatred!

Then He continued and the people weren't making it easy on Him, spats flew His way and even more cursing, they were a few women crying... very few indeed, the sad people of this earth in this cruel procession is almost non-existent.

Jesus falls again, His once beautiful knees are beaten almost to the bone, and the cross is so heavy... again I'm there watching all this happening, but even though I'm in shock in my mind, I'm looking everywhere for the Cyrene helper to carry the cross, the logical thing is for me to help Him but for some reason I couldn't.

Jesus walks a little further when he falls for the 3rd time, now this is when a man from Cyrene came and helped Him carry the Cross, it was such a cruel road to where the Romans crucified Him, I was given this Knowledge, the great Mercy that our Lord has shown to the world besides His passion and resurrection was establishing His Church in Rome showing Mercy to His assassins.

I was also given the Knowledge that this three falls from our Lord were in fact the 3 great schisms, the western schism as the first fall, the second schism with Martin Luther and the protestant reform and the Great one to come near the end... but like Ecclesiastes 1:9 "*What has been, that will be; what has been done, that will be done. Nothing is new under the sun.*" The Romans crucify Him once and are trying hard to crucify Him again and this time they want Him dead for good.

Francis: "Sharing our experience in carrying that cross, to expel the illness within our hearts, which embitters our life: it is important that you do this in your meetings. Those that are Christian, with the Bible, and those that are Muslim, with the Quran.

The faith that your parents instilled in you will always help you move on."

http://www.harvestingthefruit.com/pope-francis-encouraged-muslims-to-find-hope-in-the-quran-11-things-to-know-and-share/

Christ entrusted us to make disciples of all nations (Mark 16:15), Francis has failed Jesus to proclaim the truth in which only through Jesus we could go to the Father, He has failed the Muslims as well, because they didn't hear the truth, they heard that the faith their parents shared with them will help you move on... we all want to go to heaven and moving on to hell isn't pretty, Francis didn't proclaim the truth in Jesus and those poor souls are in danger of eternal damnation.

Why this fascination about hiding Jesus and hiding His truth? Jesus is less man in the Coran than Muhammad; a golden opportunity was missed when Francis showed more ambiguity, what would happen if one of those Muslims dies and goes to hell? Those souls would be on Francis head.

Praying for Francis isn't easy these days, not because I don't want to, but because of all his efforts to throw away the apostolic teachings of the gospel, Francis was called to proclaim ALL the truth of the gospel, not just half-truths...

The true meaning of Coran is Love Francis says, when the Coran clearly shows that all nonbelievers must be killed! Where are the true followers of Chris? Where are His true disciples? We need holiness from our priests and they are hard to find.

About the vision of the passion? Yes very few were lamenting His death... when finally the man from Cyrene arrived I understood this calmly, the Cyrene man plus the very few people lamenting through the streets, seeing their Lord walking to the Golgotha and those who didn't ran away at the foot of the cross, represents the REMNANT CHURCH, this is the church who console Jesus in this time of tribulation and new crucifixion/apostasy by the Romans.

May you see clearly what is at stake here... your eternity, which only comes through the truth in Jesus who give us the knowledge of the apostolic teachings in the Gospel, may you find peace in this turmoil, may you find Jesus and show Him to the world without fear. Amen.

Francis Cheerers: Open letter...

Hello my brethren, I want to reach out to you, Christians... who don't believe in the signs of times, who think that letting people be "happy" is letting them do whatever they want despite what God has written in His Holy bible about their wicked behavior.

Happiness is only achieve by Loving the Lord in ALL His commandments (John 14:15).

More than 75% of the Catholic Church believe in one or other evil: That homosexuality is not a sin, that contraception IS the right thing to do, that divorce and remarried should get the Eucharist and that abortion is a right.

75% is a conservative figure, because... it is actually a bigger number, even people who look Pious and Holy thinks that the Church needs to update to the times, when...

"Jesus is the same yesterday and today and forever." Heb 13:8

Most of the Church loves when our Pastors speak and behave in a "more update version" in contrast with what happened 2000 years ago, Judas DID behave like that, Judas DID the "pastoral thing" while NOT touching the Law.

Judas despite having the Word Incarnated in front of Him couldn't change Jesus and Jesus didn't change Him, as Judas did what most of the World would've done... betray Him.

There IS a reason why Sodom and Gomorrah WERE DESTROYED (Gen 19), there is a reason why the first man who used contraception God took his life, when he spilled his sperm in order NOT to give a woman a baby (Gen 38:8-10)... but people today think:

"That was then and this is now... the history doesn't apply to us."

THE RATIO OF PEOPLE INSIDE THE CHURCH BETRAYING OUR LORD HAS REACH PAST APOSTASY AND IT HAS BEEN SAID BY THEM: "DOGMA WILL STAY THE SAME..." BUT WE KNOW, THE "PASTORAL" WILL BE DONE WHILE IGNORING DOGMA.

Has Jesus EVER ignored one single coma of the Law in order to please people?

No... But today is all "Joy" and "marveling" on Mercy provided by he who is friends with the World: Francis...

Francis would've been formally excommunicated while being like this in the time of St. Pious V, St. Pope Leo the great or St. Ambrose... but today's thinking is: that was then and it is time for "Mercy."

Mercy without Justice is a falsity and Justice without Mercy the same, they both come from Divine Love, not from a source who preaches "Live and let live"

You, who love your Catholic Church... I challenge you to check History, each and every time that the Church had 2 popes, one was true the other false and the ONLY time that a pope renounce, it was pope Celestine who was advised by his closest adviser and once he resigned the adviser became pope and this man put in prison his old boss, St. pope Celestine.

Every time 2 popes are alive, one is an antipope and the other one suffers, the one suffering while "away" has always prove to be the true pope.

The adviser (Benedetto), who became pope and persecuted St Celestine, after both of them died, a new pope came and tried to pass judgment on

Benedetto as a heretic, but couldn't find proof (They were trying Benedetto as a homosexual after death), today "pope" Benedetto legacy is forgotten but pope Celestine is a Saint.

When "pope" Francis went to the EU parliament, the US congress and the UN assembly didn't mentioned the name of Jesus not once, on the contrary, he fulfilled another prophecy:

"I have come in my Father's name, and you do not accept me; but if someone else comes in his own name, you will accept him." John 5:43

"Pope" Francis speech to the UN on a Friday when our Lord died, exactly at 33 seconds in his speech:

"Thank you for your kind words. Once again, following a tradition by which I feel honored, the Secretary General of the United Nations has invited the Pope to address this distinguished assembly of nations. IN MY OWN NAME, and that of the entire Catholic community, I wish to express to you, Mr Ban Ki-moon, my heartfelt gratitude."

The World loves their own (John 15:19) and this man is Loved AND ACCEPTED, when each of the past popes were HATED, even St John Paul II despite loved inside the Church was hated everywhere.

You who likes to cheer, who don't see the signs of the times, who are blind to this man charisma, will see after this Synod the greatest schism ever to be unfold, ALL because of the "Pastoral solutions"

After Judas did his pastoral solution he died in his sin, in other words, after Francis proclaims: "I will do what my Bishops ask of me" and ignore the law but accept the pastoral wrong, all those wicked Bishops will be no longer part of the Mystical body of Jesus, so when those who Love Jesus in ALL His commands proclaim Schism, if you stay with those who betrayed our Lord in their "pastoral solutions", you will share their sin.

Francis bashed the healthiest order in the Catholic Church, the Franciscans of the Immaculate fulfilling St Francis prophecy in so many levels... but still many won't believe.

After the Pastoral solution what you'll do it is up to you... but those who DID recognize the signs, those who FLED in time, those who stood by the true pope... their reward will be bigger than most people.

We are NOT forming another Church, instead we remain FAITHFUL, we are RESISTING and ready to head into the desert knowing what lies ahead... Martyrdom.

May Jesus lets you see in time Cheerers... because Mercy without repentance is just a lie from hell, a lie that it's been sold around like the most beautiful thing and people are enjoying it.

OPEN your eyes to the truth, a Friday and 33 seconds into a speech and instead of proclaiming Jesus, proclaims honors to him... wake up brethren, wake up.

Blessings.

LETTER TO ALL FIGHTING FOR THE APOSTOLIC, CATHOLIC TRUTH.

As Holy Scripture said: *Then he returned to his disciples and said to them, "Are you still sleeping and taking your rest? Behold, the hour is at hand when the Son of Man is to be handed over to sinners. Get up, let us go. Look, my betrayer is at hand." Then all the disciples deserted Him and fled. Matthew* 26:45-46, 56.

The disciples fled ALL, not because they didn't love our Lord... they fled out of fear; but how could this also be applied to this troubled times?

When it says: "the hour is at hand when the Son of Man is to be handed over to sinners" is just that in this days... The Eucharist will be given to the most wicked sinners, those who do not want to leave their sin, those that wants to persist in the most EVIL of perversions... in Argentina we witnessed this, but it'll NOT stop there... it'll get WORST.

When it says: "Get up, let us go!" is for us and ALL who want to unite in the fight, the good fight for the love of the TRUTH OF JESUS LAID IN THE APOSTOLIC TEACHING, by proclaiming the gospel of Jesus, NOT a gospel of the world as the kumbaya gospel of Bergoglio.

BROTHERS... rise up!

When it says: "The traitor is about to arrive." Note that a traitor is someone who knows you and gives you the knowing you uses you stabbing your back for their own agenda, "Muslims with the Koran, with the faith of their fathers that it'll take them far" This is just plain false Mercy, pure Freemasonry stuff, enmity with God's people and His mandates... The traitor IS ALREADY HERE!

When it says: "Then all the disciples deserted him and fled." Question... what would've happened if the disciples had stayed? They would've been arrested and killed... How do I know? Mark 14:51-52"Now a young man followed him wearing nothing but a linen cloth about his body. They seized him, but he left the cloth behind and ran off naked."

So in these TIMES WE SHOULD FLEE WHEN THEY CHANGE THE APOSTOLIC TEACHINGS, IF THEY GIVE THE EUCHARIST TO THE SINNERS AS IT JESUS SAYS IN SAN MATTHEW 26... THAT HE WILL BE DELIVERED BY A TRAITOR TO THE SINNERS...

Do know that immediately after the schism foretold by many saints and apparitions will occur, so immediately we see this know that as well as the apostles fled, we too have to FLEE.

Open your eyes, there are many talking about loyalty and false mercy, they say: "We should not be divided, but united, Bergoglio is a saint already and he is Peter", but know this...

In reality he is a freemason because only masons accepts other denominations without trying to convert them, see his fruits with other religions and ask yourselves: Does he tries to convert them?...

Division is provided by the word of God, dividing the sheep from the goats...

Open your eyes to the truth!... The truth will change, as it right now communion to the divorced and re-married it's been practiced silently, they will say: "we shall give it to the 'weak'...", looking to be merciful, open your eyes!

Blessings...

<u>Testimony</u>

One Night I was preparing myself to pray for the whole world, for them to convert through the Mercy of our Lord Jesus.

I began to pray at 1 am... Immediately after I started, all around the sky in front of my eyes, lights big and small started to descend in front of me, I was afraid at the beginning but bit by bit I was filled with enormous joy, I kept doing my prayers and they went back to heaven again.

The next night I was about to do the same thing but this time in front of me appeared dark spots, shadows, big and small, more darker than the night itself, I was so frightened I began to shake, this shadows kept coming closer and closer, then I took out the chaplet of Archangel St. Michael, all this dark spots and shadows began to flee like a shoal of fish.

God bless His prince, St Michael the Archangel. Amen.

Open Letter to His Excellency Bp. Bernard Fellay (SSPX)

My Dear Bishop Fellay Superior General of the SSPX, your Excellency...

I am someone who was baptized in the chapel of St. Pious X in Santo Domingo, Dominican Republic, my whole childhood I didn't know who St. Pious was because, then and nowadays in our Church, the lives of the Saints and forefathers are no longer taught actively.

Through the years I grew to think that my Novus Ordo mass was excellent and everything that came from the Hierarchy was indeed with the sole intention to save my soul and lit my desire to become a saint.

Today we are seeing global apostasy and seeing priests who no longer desire to suffer in the name of Christ, the notion of Martyrdom have been lost and how those who speak the truth are being punished.

For years I didn't knew that a mass called "Tridentine" existed, but God waited for me to grow just a little bit, to show me such beauty… I have no desire to go back to the Novus Ordo mass ever again, unfortunately, I live in a place where the Bishop is no fan of the tridentine mass and my family doesn't want to hear a language they don't understand, so I have to take them there to receive the Eucharist, you see, we are suffering all around the world the relaxation of the traditions of the one true faith.

I just heard what the man seated in the Throne of Peter said about the SSPX and his "forgiveness", so that the SSPX can administer the sacrament of confession.

I remember your words in 2013 when you stated how scared to death you were with this "Genuine Modernist"…

The whole point about Vatican II was to open the gates of relaxation to souls, so that they became with less tremble and fear for God and we see this everywhere.

Your excellency, God had so much Mercy for me that He showed me in time the Latin mass, He has shown me that Sainthood starts with a 'yes' on one's part, a yes that goes towards God and His commands like the yes of our Blessed Mother, and in that yes all of us need to grow... but it is a yes to God, not to the world, watch out for those who are friends of the world, like Francis.

Please be careful with this man who is giving you a hook for you to bite, no Love for Jesus commands are in Francis deeds and words, he wants you to let down you guard and embrace His False Mercy agenda.

The Eucharist for him wasn't important then in Argentina and it is not important now, back then he let the curas villeros give the Eucharist away despite irregularity, which coincides with a woman who was told by him to "switch" to another church to receive the Eucharist despite living in adultery, coincides with the apostolic exhortation #47 that states: " the church is not a tollhouse" and "nor should the doors of the sacraments be closed by ANY reason"... all this coincides with bishops appointed by Him... who have declared that the Eucharist will NOT be negated to some dubious people, and finally coincides with Card. Walter Kasper (the Cardinal who does theology while "kneeling"), promoting "pastoral solutions" for people to relax even more and run to the Abyss with a smile by rejecting true repentance.

Your Excellency, please be very careful with this man who only calls to repentance on those who preach the truth and the beauty of Catholicism in the traditions taught by our forefathers.

The world loves his own and this pope is loved indeed by all those who no longer hear the word "repent and accept Jesus as Savior", how many of his Jewish friends have been converted? How many Muslims? How many protestants? But today proselytism is nonsense.

Many needs to hear the good news of Jesus, but instead we hear lies presented as truth as the "who am I to judge" opened the doors of hell for many, look how Illinois accepted gay marriage as law with those who am I to judge words... it seems that every day there's something new from this man which murky the waters more and more.

To me he is not pope, he never was but even though, God has commanded us to pray for those who persecute us, I pray for his soul, not his intentions.

Bishop George Francis wanted to ask him what were his intentions in reality, many faithful Catholics are afraid of the schism cloud that this man has provided with his false Mercy agenda...

If modernism is the heresy of all heresies as St Pious X said, then this man is indeed a heretic in proportions never seen and with little opposition.

I am resisting this man who everyone calls pope, but there is a pope who despite what happened with the lack of an agreement, did the motu propio, defrocked 600 pedophiles, told homosexuals that they cannot be priests, told the truth about the Muslims, sat down with you - your excellency and lifted the SSPX excommunications... Benedict XVI was a courageous pope, that's why he was pushed out.

When pope Benedict XVI said "that his power doesn't go beyond the door of his office" and when he said that he felt "alone", alone because of most priests giving their backs to him... in His abdication we see the beginning of the Fleeing to the desert like St Athanasius did and your SSPX is.

We see global apostasy and the top is in agreement with those powers, all we need to do is check the fruits... relaxation was the name of the game in the Vatican II mess and for the Church of today, this relaxation agenda, is being push harder and harder... those are his bad fruits, fruits with a little truth sprinkled with lots and lots of ambiguity (and flat out lies - don't behave like rabbits).

I was raised in the Novus Ordo and I applaud you and the SSPX to tell people to stay away from the mass which was permitted by Heaven to separate the chaff from the wheat, still, the Eucharist in the N.O. mass becomes the Flesh of God, but I know that most parts of the mass are there to dishonor God, like back then to the road of Calvary when Jesus was punched, mocked, beaten, spat and left chunks of His Holy Flesh and Blood in the streets for the health of many.

I love you in Jesus Christ your Excellency, <u>be careful</u> please... I will never think differently about you or the SSPX despite not having one here in St Petersburg FL and the negative propaganda of some... I hope this letter gets to you, I hope God gives you tons of Mercy, courage and perseverance always to withstand the hypocrisy and persecution all around us. Your flock needs you my dear man of God, it is my hope that soon rather than later, all of us in the Novus Ordo disastrous world, we go back to God in the traditions taught and pray in this dark times for the desire to become Martyrs.

Blessings...

The example of John

After the last supper Jesus went to the Gethsemane He took along the sons of Zebedee (John and James), Peter and there apart from them kneeling he prayed. Mat 26:37

John didn't understood what the Lord was saying when he dipped the morsel and gave it to Judas because how could you? After hearing the most beautiful sound in all creation... the sound of Jesus heart beating for all mankind... I mean how could he not be distracted? First it was," Master who is it" and then trying to enjoy that beautiful sound.

At the Gethsemane Jesus was praying to Almighty Father, at the same time all wheels were in motion, Judas the traitor was about to appear...

All three were sleeping, Jesus always took those three everywhere (transfiguration) and they were sleeping as the traitor got near, Jesus told them to follow Him in prayer but they decided to sleep instead, the Lord calls for something, but man follows their desires... "The spirit is willing but the flesh is weak." Mat 26:41

John woke up to find that Jesus was to be apprehended by the Jews and now sees the traitor with them, now he realizes that Judas was the one who Jesus said was going to betray Him.

The one who Jesus love, fled the scene for a totally different reason than all the rest, yes indeed, all Apostles fled including him, but he ran where? To Jesus Mother... Mary; after this, you could see John stuck like glue to our Holy Mother Mary, everywhere She went during Jesus passion, John was there to witness...

And that beautiful sound? An ocean of Mercy pounding for all mankind, that sweet sound in Jesus heart was Mary the Queen of Mercy... This is why John fled, he didn't felt fear like all the rest, he went to retrieve the Queen of Mercy as She too had to suffer as co-redemtrix for all mankind. Luke 2:35

Mary is Mercy in human form, Her Mercy lies in Her blessed womb: Jesus.

I'm writing this words at 3:07 am and my heart is filled with beautiful Mercy... John heard Mercy and took that Mercy to His house, Mary the Queen of Mercy is the weapon of choice by Almighty Father in this end times, as Her Rosary and the Scapular will save the world fulfilling prophecy. 1 Sam 17:40

The example of John in this end times (were confusion and lies are presented like candy by our own clergy), this example is important to persevere in truth, now you have to ask this question: do most priests, bishops and cardinals have taken Mary into their homes? Have they rush in the sad hour to get Mary like John did? Can you see in them a past history of consistency devoted to Mary as John did?

This is why John was the loved one, Jesus saw true dedication to the priesthood through Mary.

John went out to seek Mary, he took Her into his house and kept listening the most beautiful sound from Jesus own heart, that sound: our Mother, our Captain the Queen of Mercy, Mary who wants you to embrace Her son in everything, like she did, John is the best example of that.

Maria, my dear Sister... (Open Letter to our dear sister MDM)

Maria, my dear Sister...

My dear Sister, I am not the one who should address you because I am a worthless man, someone who is a remnant wanna be.

Nevertheless I'm trying to do my part, trying to crawl back from the person I use to be: a blackened soul who has enjoyed the Mercy of our Savior and Lord Jesus, Mercy which has pulled me towards God's Salvation.

Way before reading the messages you received and written, I knew something was wrong when I saw Pope Benedict's resignation... I felt like something was stripped from me, I felt like 'naked' in the streets.

When Mario Bergoglio seized power, I almost cried, when saw him saying 'hi' instead of blessing us with the sign of the cross from the papal balcony, I was blind like many, despite Benedict's suffering.

Then I've heard Francis said: 'Atheists do good', 'Who am I to judge' but, what it confirmed my fears that Francis was an antipope - the false prophet, was when he fulfilled the prophecy of St. Francis of Assisi with the scourging of the Franciscans of the Immaculate.

When St. Francis of Assisi in his prophecy said "The IMMACULATE purity of our order would be eclipsed" right there, with the hammering of the Franciscans of the IMMACULATE, that prophecy was fulfilled, it opened my eyes.

At the time, I didn't know the messages you had written, only right after this bullying of the Franciscans that's when I came to know you, when William Tapley mentioned you, I had to investigate for myself...

I have heard the Voice of our Lord twice a year since 1992 and when I finally read the messages, I have heard His voice each and every time I read them... it is a joy and blessing I don't deserve. Since, I have seen a persecution that I've never imagine existed inside the one true faith, to anyone who stands for the truth, I have been blind for so long.

This is the time when I discovered many things, I didn't know the Latin mass existed, I didn't know how much suffering and persecution many prophets, seers and servants have suffered in the hands of our own due to the truth, again I have been so naive in spiritual matters, so Luke-warmth despite having been blessed by our Lord many times.

Even my mentors persecute someone, like it is a sport in our Church... but now I know that when truth is spoken, immediately after persecution starts, even in your own home.

I have seen the excuses the persecutors have in order to tell you that you are 'false' Sister, how wrong they are...

St. Paul has the first precedent in rebuking PUBLICLY an established pope, many saints have rebuke anti-popes and even good popes who started weak, but ended in sainthood due to holy people, to tell them how wrong or weak they are.

I can challenge every claim that says that you are false with the Holy bible alone, each and every message, not because I can, because God have made me seen how each message DOES stay in line with the Holy Word of God.

But I know, the messenger shouldn't be defended... only the message needs to be proclaimed and the message is not yours, but God's. YOU are the writer, the writer who suffers along with chosen souls for the salvation of souls, you are indeed the last prophet in this dark times I know because God have said so, and you can see it in the fruits, how every message is been fulfilled even though you detractors claims dates and falsities.

The lies presented as truth, is what we need to denounce, and every day there's something out there contradicting God's law, this 'contradictions' comes from the Judas clothed as Peter and many little antichrists everywhere running their local governments and nations... but even though we pray for their souls, not their intentions.

You are our sister, which God has chosen to be His last prophet, the seventh angel... poor those who put lies about you, poor Ms. Carberry who has tag along in their sick game, claiming that she is you... but I bless them despite their horrific claims... God have Mercy on their souls.

My dear sister... I love you in Jesus Christ, a big hug with sincere and innocent affection, because of your suffering and openness to God, I have been led to pray the Rosary many times daily, the

Chaplet, to go to confession more, never to miss mass... all of this to me was lukewarmth before; praying for the salvation of souls have been a bitter sweet task because of the persecution, but God has promised to be with all of us and that gives me peace.

It doesn't matter the fingers, it is not worth our time defending you, on the contrary, we rejoice in this bitter persecution, as God have allow us to suffer in the name of Christ.

Blessings to those who disagree with us... we are exercising our right to resist and resisting is not a lack of Love or disobedience, it is love trying to wake people up so souls can be saved.

Despite whatever the cost, move forth Sister... we are praying, we are enduring suffering, we are sacrificing... there is a precedent in the lives of the saints and forefathers for the things your persecutors points their fingers at you... even those servants who have, but claimed that they don't know if homosexuality is a sin, it is just sad.

Sadness, yes it is sad seeing so much apostasy, sadness having persecution in your own home, land, and within relatives...

But tons of Joy in His Divine Mercy for allowing us to live in this critical times.

Tons of Blessings for you, your family and the Remnant Army everywhere... go forth latter day Saints...

All the Power, Love and Glory to God the Father, our Lord and Savior Jesus, and the Holy Spirit forever. Amen

Mother of Salvation pray for us. Amen

Joey Lomangino, the Knight of Garabandal has gone to heaven

(Please say a Hail Mary for Him and Mari Loli)

Today sad and joyful news came to our ears, Joey Lomangino (http://www.garabandal.us/joey-lomangino-padre-pio/) the knight of Garabandal has died, confirmed today by friends, family, and Conchita González to Glenn Hudson a longtime friend and volunteer in the Garabandal center of NYC.

It is truly sad for the entire world that Joey is no longer with us, many may wonder right away about his sight, but those who knew him better are not worried about that, their hearts are in grief and sadness like many of us Catholics who are no longer with him.

Sadness I felt right away as I began to read about his death…

Immediately I wondered about His sight and the Miracle, doubts came knocking on my door and I had the sadness now mixed with doubts and uncertainty about this apparition... but all of the sudden the thought of Joey opening his eyes to our Blessed Mother smiling while passing to the other world lit my heart with something so beautiful that my doubts went away and the sadness disappeared.

Joey fought the world as a blind man, but he knew he wasn't going to be blind eternally, and with a smile he showed us sacramentals from Garabandal kissed and blessed by our Mother for years; hope wasn't lost, because hope was all in him, as Joey saw the Miracle with permission of Heaven and his eyes restored to see the most beautiful smile... from our Holy Mother.

Faith is all right now in this time of darkness, our Love for Jesus Christ to fight the world, as we dream and hope of the new world to come in Heaven, the warning and miracle is fast approaching, as God promised through our Lady to Conchita, Mari Loli, Jacinta, Mari Cruz, passed down to Garabandal's soldier Joey Lomangino and to all the world.

Sadness yes because we lost Joey, but pure Joy as he walks happy towards our Mother welcoming him to Her Son's Kingdom, my heart is happy to see you in such a wonderful company Joey...

Jesus and Mary are by your side now with Fr Pio smiling from a corner holding the hand of Mari Loli... I Love you in Christ Joey, may Jesus keep you in His open side for eternity and give tons of Mercy to your family, and to all of Garabandal's soldiers out there in which you were an example of a "Yes" like our Blessed Lady said Yes. Amen

Testimony

I was one time in Gethsemane I saw the Lord being taken by the enemy, immediately I saw how the ear of slave was cut by the sword of one of the disciples, Jesus put His hands on to the slave and a new ear was formed.

Jesus was taken all the disciples disappear into the night, they went in front of the High priest but all the way there he was mocked and beaten, and the poor slave wanted to do something but did not.

He was put in an unfair trial, the slave was seeing all this, his master was judging the Lord of Lords, but he couldn't do anything, he didn't say anything.

Then all of the sudden I was taken to the outside where the Lord was waiting for me, I asked my Lord 'Lord Jesus who am I resemble more in my life, the slave or Peter?'

Lord Jesus said to me: 'You resemble more Peter.'

Immediately I was brought back to reality, I knew the Lord wasn't saying Peter as all the good things Peter had, but I felt it was that Peter who betrayed Him...

I felt bad and sad... but if I trust you Lord, you will make me a better man, and instead of a hypocrite, traitor, liar, murderer, thief and all the bad things you know I am Jesus, I want to trust you more, please save me Lord, save from drowning in my own iniquities, save me from me. Amen

Tears of St. Petersburg

Please before reading this, do know we don't have one gram of hate towards Bishop Lynch, and we pray you ask heaven strength to avoid hate, we ask you to pray for this man (not his intentions) so he can embrace Christ with a sincere and repentant heart.

Wolves in sheep clothing are all around us and the demise of the faith is the new trend, we can see this in the Tampa Bay area where the Bishop allows iniquity to take place and denies the hunger for our Lord.

The teaching of our Church has been clear forever, homosexuals and wicked people are welcome to the Church, but they need to repent and convert as well, the relatio says that the Church doesn't welcome sinners.

"The Kingdom of God is at hand, repent and believe in the Gospel" Mark 1:15

This man and all wolves in sheep clothing, clearly needs our prayers to convert and embrace Jesus entirely; in the year 2000 shut down perpetual adoration to our Lord, no wonder, he is more known as a charismatic individual (peoples man) rather than a spiritual man.

Bishop Robert Lynch canceled the perpetual adoration of the Lord in his entire diocese, is been 14 years since that abomination took place...

"Keep your eyes fixed upon Jesus, who inspires and perfects our faith" --Hebrews 12:2

Those who seek have to wait one day out of the week and for 3 hours adore, if it is in St. Jude parish is little bit longer, but the damage has been there for long as reports from the laity is coming out that some St. Petersburg priests are turning off the A/C and the lights for people to be discourage and continue adoration, thanks Bishop Lynch.

I'm not going to the Schiavo (picture above) failure of his, the Miracle washed by his orders in that building in Clearwater, or he admitting through that 150k payout that something very wrong happened... no; the relatio came out with a lie from hell and to no surprise he was super happy... as the **relatio was the most honest** thing he has read out of this Synod.

He said once that there's finally a shift, and Mr. Voris wondered what he was referring to, now we know:

Liberalism have finally arrived and the wolves are salivating, seeing, soon they won't have to hide in sheep's clothing anymore, don't worry Bishop Lynch, we know... for your sake and the flock you were given to... REPENT AND BELIEVE IN THE GOSPEL, not just a tiny piece but everything as a whole, accept Jesus... surrender to His marvelous and Just Kingship. Amen.

Blessings.

Prayer for all persecuted Christians

(Please Pray)

Eternal Father, I offer Thee the Most Precious Blood of Thy Divine Son, Jesus, in union with the masses said throughout the world today, for all the holy souls in purgatory, for sinners everywhere, for sinners in the universal church, those in my own home and within my family. Amen.

A Hail Mary and Glory follows.

Then the prayer to Almighty Father for all persecuted Christians:

Almighty Father, Father of Mercy, Father of all comfort, Yahweh King of the heavenly armies, I beg You for the most holy wounds of your Son our Lord Jesus Christ that You send Your Strong Arm to protect all around the world who is persecuted by the world powers, the powers of the devil and his minions; people persecuted because of their voice and example which testifies of the good news of Jesus and Your Kingdom, people who love more than their own lives Your only begotten Son in whom You are well pleased, send your strong arm:

Archangel St. Michael, Archangel St. Gabriel, Archangel St. Raphael and all the guardian angels to protect them, I beg You Lord for the wounds of Thy most Holy Son. Amen.

Immediately after you need to pray the Chaplet of St. Michael Archangel…

O God, come to my assistance. O Lord, make haste to help me. Glory be to the Father, etc.

[Say one Our Father and three Hail Marys after each of the following nine salutations in honor of the nine Choirs of Angels]

1. By the intercession of St. Michael and the celestial Choir of Seraphim may the Lord make us worthy to burn with the fire of perfect charity.
Amen.

2. By the intercession of St. Michael and the celestial Choir of Cherubim may the Lord grant us the grace to leave the ways of sin and run in the paths of Christian perfection.
Amen.

3. By the intercession of St. Michael and the celestial Choir of Thrones may the Lord infuse into our hearts a true and sincere spirit of humility.
Amen.

4. By the intercession of St. Michael and the celestial Choir of Dominations may the Lord give us grace to govern our senses and overcome any unruly passions.
Amen.

5. By the intercession of St. Michael and the celestial Choir of Virtues may the Lord preserve us from evil and falling into temptation. Amen.

6. By the intercession of St. Michael and the celestial Choir of Powers may the Lord protect our souls against the snares and temptations of the devil.
Amen.

7. By the intercession of St. Michael and the celestial Choir of Principalities may God fill our souls with a true spirit of obedience. Amen.

8. By the intercession of St. Michael and the celestial Choir of Archangels may the Lord give us perseverance in faith and in all good works in order that we may attain the glory of Heaven.
Amen.

9. By the intercession of St. Michael and the celestial Choir of Angels may the Lord grant us to be protected by them in this mortal life and conducted in the life to come to Heaven.
Amen.

Say one Our Father in honor of each of the following leading Angels: St. Michael, St. Gabriel, St. Raphael and our Guardian Angel.

Concluding prayers:

O glorious prince St. Michael, chief and commander of the heavenly hosts, guardian of souls, vanquisher of rebel spirits, servant in the house of the Divine King and our admirable conductor, you who shine with excellence and superhuman virtue deliver us from all evil, who turn to you with confidence and enable us by your gracious protection to serve God more and more faithfully every day.

Pray for us, O glorious St. Michael, Prince of the Church of Jesus Christ, that we may be made worthy of His promises.

Almighty and Everlasting God, Who, by a prodigy of goodness and a merciful desire for the salvation of all men, has appointed the most glorious Archangel St. Michael Prince of Your Church, make us worthy, we ask You, to be delivered from all our enemies, that none of them may harass us at the hour of death, but that we may be conducted by him into Your Presence. This we ask through the merits of Jesus Christ Our Lord. Amen.

Mother Courageous

One of my favorite phrases from the bible is Apocalypse 12:1, "Behold, a sign in the sky, a woman clothed with the sun, with the moon under her feet and a crown of twelve stars." I see the moon at night and I think about it, think about my mother, our captain, the Holy Virgin Mary.

I remember that most people talk about the woman in this chapter as the Church, which is true, it is the Church, but at the same time in the literal sense of view... it is Mary.

The Holy Scripture is a double edge sword and apocalypse 12:2 continues: "And being with child, she cried travailing in birth, and was in pain to be delivered." Our Mother had pain, but she was sinless so she didn't need to delivered the child with pain because of Her state of grace she was spared, but **our Mother is the most courageous woman ever created and she chose pain to delivered the Child... it is written: "and was in pain to be delivered."**

Our Catholic Church is not mistaken, she is sinless so she could delivered without pain, but not Mary, the proof of her courage is the most beautiful "yes" ever said to God, despite what would've happened to Her if they knew she was with a child and no man, that was a death sentence right there, but she said yes to that pain, because she suffered that situation too.

She suffered not because she could've died, she suffered like so many prophets and seers had to endure as well, most people would've doubt, but not Her!

She delivered the King of Kings and she chose to have this pain, this pain that every mother has to suffer, and she became the model for victim souls on how to accept the will of God and choosing suffering instead of worldly things in order to please God, and it was God who gave Her this options, do you really think that if she prays to God for her to be spared of pain, God in His Mercy would've said no? She chose pain and delivered the King in the midst of this unique pain that all mothers know only.

And Apocalypse continues in 12:6... "And the woman fled into the wilderness, where she had a place prepared by God, that there they should feed her a thousand two hundred sixty days."

John the most beloved disciple took the woman into his home, his home is the Church as this disciple is a priest and the Woman who in this passage is both the Church and our Lady, the Holy Virgin Mary, is persecuted into the desert or wilderness, that right there is the remnant Church as the disciple John took Her so this remnant Church will be also those who love Her and the persecution will be ferocious, but in the end Her immaculate heart will triumph.

Most people don't love Her anymore, most priests that are Her servants are persecuted and ridiculed, and all she wants us to do is to please Her son our Lord Jesus Christ, most Catholics today preferred a simple prayer over the rosary, when the Rosary IS the weapon of choice in this end times, those who love Her truly, they do advance spiritually because of Her favors as explain in psalm 45.

Our Lady is the most courageous woman ever created and still is, despite a lot of Her Children denying Her, but soon will come the hour that many will call to Her for salvation and that salvation lies only in the Blessed fruit of Her womb, Jesus.

Mother Mary I love you!

My first Heavenly dream

Even though I went to a Catholic school, I wasn't a good Catholic, this is my first dream with heavenly things...

"I was sitting in a dark room waiting for something, but that something I didn't know what it was; in front of me there was a huge double door and to my right a single small door..."

"Suddenly the double door opens and I could see many people inside, there was so many people that they were standing one on top of each other, enjoying themselves..."

"It was like a huge discotheque, everybody was drinking, dancing, talking, screaming, laughing and it was so packed that it felt like they were inside of can, like fish..."

"Then this place invited me to go in, but my soul was frightened, telling me that we shouldn't go..."

"This place was packed and even though there was an apparent joy, my soul felt so frightened to go in that I wasn't moving"

"I noticed that people was they went in, they couldn't step out... The place was so packed, but no one could step outside..."

"Then I realize that this was hell... A mirage was placed like a veil in front of my eyes so I could see joy instead of what it really was... This place was calling me even harder, telling me that I belong there."

"I was afraid to go in, but I couldn't stay on the bench or seat where I was... so I stood up and didn't want to go in..."

"Then I ran to the little door to my right, thinking "I deserve hell, I'm trespassing heaven"....

"My soul was right this was heaven indeed, nobody stop me from going in so I guess is alright..."

"All was white, big halls, like a mansion I've never seen... I kept walking and to my left there was this huge door..."

"I went in and I'm shock to see the Virgin Mary crying profusely... I was petrified seen Her in such profound pain, I couldn't move, I couldn't do anything for her."

"Then in an instant I was taken back to earth and I woke up..."

You could have dreams during your life time and all could fade away into oblivion, I was 15 years old maybe 16 I'm not quite sure on that, but I remember and I'm never forgetting that dream... at the time I Knew that I wasn't deserving of heaven but I went in and nobody there stop me... out of Mercy I was in, but until today I didn't know much what that dream meant, and this is what it means:

You decide to go to hell... not God, you, He just passes judgment on you, your actions will reflect eternally, nobody deserves heaven, but the ones who seek holiness shall receive Mercy and their sins will be erased...

We all shall seek perfection through a YES on our part, nobody is forced to accept God's way, it's either heaven or hell YOU CHOOSE, now after you choose heaven a time will pass were you'll suffer in the waiting room (life) where you will suffer (remember how much pain I suffered knowing I did deserve hell even though I wanted heaven).

My soul was right, but it was what was given to my soul telling me to be very afraid of wrongdoing, very afraid to displease God as all other souls didn't want to go to heaven; I did went only after I REJECTED the WORLD and its offerings, I REJECTED HELL AT THE SAME TIME...

Today after 25 years I know why I saw our Lady crying, because it was like the WHOLE EARTH REJECTED HEAVEN, THE ENTIRE WORLD WAS PLUNGING TO HELL...

I'm not yet Holy but I want to say yes, I'm not merciful or humble, I'm not a saint and still Jesus chose me for something, I want to please Him and tell the whole world about His Mercy, which is Love in action, Love from the OFFENDED to the AGRESSOR which is me and you...

I have long ways to go through His pain and Love I will be taught, because His Lord, King and Master, from this unworthy me I want to die a Martyr for the Gospel and Him, but 1st we need to learn how to be Humble, how to be merciful, and how to please Jesus according to His commands...

I know that I'm speaking against someone in the church, Jesus never told me to do that but He never STOPPED me... To receive Mercy Yes, now to be merciful... follow the Gospel of who rejoices with truth and hates iniquity (psalm 45) be perfect like our Father in heaven is perfect, like Jesus taught us when He was giving His life as an example, His commandments are the way, He said to the adulterer "I'm not judging you, BUT don't sin again"

Let's reject together the world and this apostates who wants a worldly church build in false Mercy, because Mercy without Justice is like Love without truth and that is just ambiguous, is Jesus ambiguous? Deny ourselves, deny Hell/the world and let's give our lives for the Gospel. Amen

<u>Testimony</u>

Conversation between my good friend Mickey Duran and me, this happened to me several years ago on a train in New York...

Abandon yourself to Jesus... I say it's not the same knowing Who He is, than knowing as you and I know each other...

Look what happened to me one day in the subway train going from Manhattan to Harlem I was thinking about Jesus in my mind, I was thinking how great is His love and hear this...I was standing on that train, suddenly I felt a hand going inside my chest, hear this... IT ENTERED MY CHEST!

HE did NOT touch my chest... Jesus entered His hands inside my chest touching my heart. I felt it all, each and every one of HIS BEAUTIFUL FINGERS, Jesus touched the inside of my heart.

As He did this, I had to hold STRONGLY to the train from keeping me from falling... I held my tears, because of His Sweetness entering my heart, I didn't know what would've become of me with such beauty in that train.

I arrived to my stop and the feeling of love remained in my heart for a long time...

Very few people know this happened to me that day on that train, heading to my sister's house.

JESUS lives, He is real and has tons of Mercy for whom with a sincere and humble heart, asks for His Mercy, but His sweet Mercy DOESN'T CONDONE sins.

"Be perfect as your heavenly Father is perfect" (Matthew 5:48) The Father loves the sinner but love DOESN'T CONDONE the stubbornness, He forgives those who ask sincere forgiveness, a heartfelt REPENTENCE makes perversion to flee.

Blessings.

I CRIED WHEN I WROTE THIS..

Blessed are the prostitutes who repent with a sincere heart and embrace My Heart, the door of heaven I'll open for them...

Blessed are drug users who leave their needles in my hands for forgiveness, on that day, my tears will cleansed their souls...

Blessed the repentant homosexuals, who sought my forgiveness and found it in my side; there, in their surrender to chastity, I will teach them to deny the world, taking the fingers pointing to them as part of their cross and the day to day walk in my tracks will show them the purity that they need, then at the end, they will find rest beside me in the Golgotha, there will overcome through me, recognizing me as their Lord.

Blessed are those who decide to follow my commandments and endure all manner of persecution, in suffering they will hear Me: "Smile soon we will be in paradise"

Blessed are those who love truth and shout it without fear, doubts will disappear and the test will teach them temperance.

Blessed my priests who suffer, weep, laugh and sacrifice for love to their Lord, that same sadness and joy in My service will be their card I'll take to my Heavenly Father...

Blessed My priests who are eager to bring me souls through the road I taught, in them, I rejoice...

Blessed my priests who know how to use everything I gave them to defeat hell, they will have no fear of being in the entrance of Hades and save my flock.

Blessed he who overcomes fear in favor of spreading my gospel, for these are those which I referred in the mount:

"Blessed are they who hunger and thirst for righteousness, for they will be satisfied"

Blessed is my remnant Church that sees horror and is not frightened, because she knows I'm with her and like a jealous Bridegroom will defend her from all iniquity.

Woe to those who know the truth and don't want to follow,

Woe to those who sells the promise out of fear in this test times...

Woe to those who in these trouble times, sold the promise out of fear,

Woe unto those wicked and manipulative priests, for hell is around them and they will die for their injustice.

My Church! Remember my commandments..!

Priests of mine! Learn from me, for I am meek and humble of heart, my yoke is easy and my burden light!

Praying the Chaplet is an error?

Have you ever heard: that the Divine Mercy chaplet is bad and wrong to pray it? You are not alone many people out there hanging out with that misconception, because this devotion was locked by two popes, but released by two popes also, everyone who says it's wrong to pray this, denies these two Popes: Paul VI and John Paul II, therefore these people do not know it yet but they have sedevacantism ink in them, granting a pope more authority than the others, it is a mistake in their part as sedevacantism, according to the saint and doctor of the Church Robert Bellermain.

(http:/ / www.youtube.com/watch?v=1UUcVisQcLk) it's an ERROR.

Whoever likes practicing the Divine Mercy devotion go ahead and do it, it's not bad on the contrary is good, nobody is saying NO to the Rosary, it'll be much better if you make them both daily, is an ERROR from the sedevacantism by saying that the crown is not good and this error has corroded many Catholics hearts.

Devotion to the Divine Mercy is good and valid, to say otherwise is from sedevacantism and sedevacantism is WRONG...

NO ONE IS HOLY, WE SHALL BE SAINTS BY THE MERCY OF JESUS ONLY, but having Mercy doesn't mean the CONDONING of sins and erase truth, those who are truly tied to the Divine Mercy this don't stand still, always knowing that after Mercy comes Justice, this is why Jesus says, "be perfect as your Father is perfect" (Matthew 5:48) but also says, "Without me, you can do nothing" (John 15:5).

We must not for one moment neglect our situation around the Mercy received, practice Mercy and Mercy in context, which is Love in Action, Love is Mercy, Justice and Truth... "Be perfect as your Father is perfect" but being perfect is impossible without Jesus and His action in us, therefore, what He taught us we must practice... in His teachings the whole truth is and practice that on behalf of our brother is Mercy, but not you can't live the beatitudes knowing that the salt which loses its flavor is skinned in the streets (Matthew 5:13).

The Divine Mercy is lived, prayed, shared, knowing that you should let yourself die, you must fully surrender to Jesus and He will be the one doing for you... the chaplet was curiously released exactly when it was most needed, right after the Vatican II disaster, so it was no coincidence that it was with papal lock until Paul VI freed all banned books and John Paul II took it under his wings, this chaplet was not made for that time of Faustina Kowalska but for this time, but sedevacantism always has something to criticize, they do not understand that the same power that had had Pious XII John Paul II had, the chaplet is good, the devotion is good...

Some sedevacantists declares that father Pio is in hell (because he did the Novus ordo), that Garabandal subsequently is of the devil, therefore, even though some popes made mistakes at the time, I do not doubt for a moment that they were popes, John XXIII didn't obey Fatima, but Mother Mary mentions him in Garabandal, Paul VI built a Mass according to the world, but he is mentioned in Garabandal, JPII kissed the Koran but he is mentioned in Garabandal, Benedict XVI is mentioned in Garabandal and in the prophecies of Pope Pious X, these popes are real and did recognized (from Paul VI onwards) the Divine Mercy devotion.

Now who abuses the Divine Mercy today? WOLVES DRESSED IN SHEEP saying that is better to respect others that's why they prefer forgive and not condemn, that's why I did not join a traditionalist newspaper which I was invited to (and I love tradition and the Latin mass more than Vatican II), but I know many traditionalists and sedevacantists and so far I have NOT found one who likes the devotion to the Divine Mercy, I consider myself a child of the Novus Ordo (because my mission is more suited to this Mass than to the Latin mass-which I like better than the N. Ordo) and I'm called to tell the world about the Mercy of Jesus, to anyone who wants to hear, the chaplet has NO defects, it is a perfect prayer that would make it even better, if prayed after the Rosary daily, yes! DAILY!

No demon would ask you to do the Rosary and then make the chaplet, now theologically: the chaplet is supported biblically, as we offer to Almighty Father the body, soul, blood and divinity of our Lord Jesus; John Paul II realized this and recommended personally to all of us to live this devotion, but he never stopped promoting the Rosary on the contrary he love it so much that he added the Luminous Mystery.

So whoever tells you that the Mercy chaplet was forbidden by two popes (Faustina's diary), immediately think of Paul VI who released the banned books and John Paul II made valid this devotion of pure love, whoever comes to you with that nonsense that it is bad to pray and follow that devotion, simply put that person in prayer and not listen to them.

Jesus could not leave His Church without this weapon for long, as Paul VI thought the church would destroy itself with self-criticism after Vatican II, the faucet of grace has been closing slowly after Vatican II and you this is true as you can see that there are no more cure of Ars and father Pio been born in the world after Vat. II, think about this, pray and you'll see it's true... way too much LIBERATION have been promoted after Vatican II by the enemies of God, promoting false mercy.

The responsibility of the one who has the devotion of Divine Mercy in their life is to pray daily for the conversion of all sinners, the Holy Virgin Mary at Fatima said that more souls go to hell for lack of prayer by us for them than anything else; so only asking Mercy for yourselves and not for the brother is like those Protestants carrying the false idea of "once saved, always saved" rather than, once saved, always saved by denying yourself, taking your daily cross and following Jesus, but where Jesus was headed when he said that? Days later He was to be crucified in the Golgotha, so we have to follow Him in persecution and in martyrdom.

Persecution and Martyrdom you will get when you pray for others, you will fall into an arduous chase by the devil, but you have Jesus and his beautiful Sweet Mother, the Rosary and the Chaplet together for the love of sinners and their conversion to the Heart of Jesus...

REJECT (fraternally) anyone who comes to you saying, that the Chaplet of Divine Mercy is wrong, it'll be wrong is if you stay ONLY in the sweetness of Mercy alone and begin to CONDONE sins for the sake of being Merciful that does NOT work! Pray for the conversion of the world, abandon yourself to Jesus, gladly accept the persecution and fear not to die for Him, martyrdom is a gift, which is heaven in a silver platter.

Blessings, St. Faustina Kowalska pray for us.

Amen.

What is the warning?

(The Warning in Holy Spcripture)

In the evening of June 18, 1961, four girls - Conchita Gonzalez, Maria Dolores (Mari-Ioli) Mazón, Jacinta Gonzalez and Maria Cruz Gonzalez, and all were from poor families.

Suddenly they heard a loud noise, and saw before them the bright figure of the Archangel Michael. He announced that on July 2 they would see Our Lady.

Conchita wrote:

"The warning comes directly from God and will be visible to the whole world and from any place where anyone many happen to be. It will be like the revelation of our sins and it will be seen and felt by everyone, believer and unbeliever alike irrespective of whatever religion he may belong to. It will be seen and felt in all parts of the world and by every person."

It will happen in the sky, no one can prevent it from happening. We will even prefer to be dead rather than to pass through this Warning It will not kill us. It will be a "correction" of our conscience. It will cause great fear and will make us reflect within ourselves on the consequences of our own personal sins. It will be like a warning of the punishment to come. In this way the world will be offered a means of purification to prepare itself for the extraordinary grace of the Great Miracle which will happen within one year after The Warning.

Jacinta was told by Our Blessed Mother:

"The warning would come when conditions were at their worst."

If we do not pay attention to the message, the punishment announced by Our Lady will be visited on the whole world after *The miracle.*

The warning in the Bible

"At midnight the cry rang out: 'Here's the bridegroom! Come out to meet him!' Matt 25:6

"And He will send his angels with a loud trumpet call, and they will gather his elect from the four winds, from one end of the heavens to the other." Matt 24:31

"Do not be amazed at this, for a time is coming when all who are in their graves will hear His voice" John 5:28

"For the Lord himself will come down from heaven, with a loud command, with the voice of the archangel and with the trumpet call of God, and the dead in Christ will rise first." 1 Thes 4:16

The Warning is described in Holy Scripture telling us beforehand that the time to fulfill Jesus second coming is right around the corner, a few moments away to judge His faithful and all nations.

Cry, loud trumpet call, all that are in their graves will hear His call and again the trumpet call of God.

These parts in Holy Scripture reveal what will happen during that time, we are focusing only about the warning revealed in Garabandal and many other seers and prophets around the world.

A cry that tells you the bridegroom is near, warns you that you must be ready for Him and if you are ready, is because you have lived and breath His commandments, in other words you have lived only trusting Him and that trust has make you a living example of holiness that comes only from Him, not you.

The Warning will be the "Great sign appeared the sky" (Rev 12:1) and at that moment the only thing that will come to your soul is GOD, He exists and Jesus is His Son, Jesus is God because the sign that you will see in the sky, will be the cross and

God will show you your sins "all who are in their graves will hear His voice" John 5:28

This showing of your sins is a gift by God called: "The illumination of conscience" soon after the Warning two things will happen in you, either you repent or you will ignore the last effort of Divine Mercy by God to accept His Son Jesus as Savior and His Hand of Salvation.

John 5:28 speaks literally, when the dead will rise up to meet the Lord, but also speaks about us dead, those submerge in sins... dead men and women walking due to our transgressions, on that day like when Lot, who waited long for God until one day receive the Angels in his house, and I can only imagine all doubts in his family crumbling down, but even though, there shall be many like Lot's wife who will turn into statues of salt for not obeying His Holy Word, lifeless.

The Warning is in the Bible and it will happen, believe it or not...

It is dark the hour now and everything will turn worst as the Catholic Church is about to embrace full apostasy fulfilling 2 Thes 2:3-4,7-12

"Don't let anyone deceive you in any way, for that day will not come until the rebellion occurs and the man of lawlessness is revealed, the man doomed to destruction. He will oppose and will exalt himself

*over everything that is called God or is worshiped,
so that he sets himself up in God's temple,
proclaiming himself to be God.*

*"For the secret power of lawlessness is already at
work; but the one who now holds it back will
continue to do so till HE is taken out of the way.
And then the lawless one will be revealed, whom
the Lord Jesus will overthrow with the breath of his
mouth and destroy by the splendor of his coming.
The coming of the lawless one will be in
accordance with how Satan works. He will use all
sorts of displays of power through signs and
wonders that serve the lie, and all the ways that
wickedness deceives those who are perishing.
They perish because they refused to love the truth
and so be saved. For this reason God sends them
a powerful delusion so that they will believe the lie
and so that all will be condemned who have not
believed the truth but have delighted in
wickedness."*

Truth… all around the world many lies have
endured throughout time and many have swallow
lies as truth, but the Catholic Church which contains
ALL the truth in Jesus, is about to embrace
apostasy and cut all ties with Heaven as the
Eucharist will be canceled soon (one who now
holds it back will continue to do so till HE is taken
out of the way 2 Thes 2:7).

Do you think everything is bad right now? Wait when the Eucharist is canceled, allowing the abomination of desolation to be established, and then the last effort of God for man to embrace Divine Mercy in His only begotten Son Jesus in the warning, will happen.

Afterwards? Pure HORROR will follow, as the chastisement and the Antichrist will be revealed. The living shall envy the dead... Garabandal was just the beginning, and recently a prophet has risen to trumpet God's second coming... so whoever has ears, LISTEN, that prophet is Maria of Divine Mercy, one of His angels who calls...

"Watch and pray that you may not undergo the test" Matt 26:41

The Illumination of Conscience

When a Light blinded St Paul, afterwards he knew Jesus was God (Acts 22:7), St. Paul immediately believed; when St. Longinus opened Jesus side with the spear, Holy Blood and Water gush out and sprinkled into Longinus face, he immediately knew, as a centurion proclaimed: "Truly this was the Son of God" (Mark 15:39)

Apostle John said so (John 19:36): "They will look to the one they pierced"

Garabandal 1961, our most Blessed Lady appeared to 4 children and left us, through them, a prophecy that has been told through many saints and the Gospel as well.

Saint Edmund Campion: "pronounced a great day, not wherein any temporal potentate should minister, but wherein the Terrible Judge should reveal all men's consciences and try every man of each kind of religion."

Blessed Elizabeth Canori-Mora: "a great light appeared upon the earth which was the 'sign of the reconciliation' of God with man."

Blessed Anna Maria Taigi had a similar vision in which she foresaw that "a great purification will come upon the world preceded by an 'illumination of conscience' in which everyone will see themselves as God sees them."

Pius IX: "There will be a great prodigy which will fill the world with awe,"

Saint Faustina saw a "great luminous Cross in the Sky" and the list goes on, in Garabandal is the same, an illumination of conscience... humans will see the state of their souls with all their transgressions against God, and every human being shall know that He (Jesus) is God.

If you go from the first page of the Bible to the last, you will notice something... promises, God's promises are always fulfilled by Him always in time according to His will, and His will is that every knee on earth, heaven and the abyss kneels before Jesus Christ. (Phil 2:10)

The world and its master doesn't want that, but that is the will of Almighty Father and His will reigns beside Him: Jesus, and He has sent us many seers and prophets in the last 30 years and they all fell into oblivion due to a wicked world and the helping hand of the Church, the Bishop of Santander didn't recognize Garabandal as "supernatural", but NOT the message, it was never condemned, but many got confused and rejected Garabandal due to our Church rejection of its supernaturality.

Now a new Prophet has come forth, Maria of Divine Mercy and she (the writer) has taken our dear and soon to embrace apostasy, Catholic Church by storm... the center of the message? God's soon to come upon us act of Mercy: the warning with the Illumination of Conscience, and... Yes, the Church is rejecting this messages.

Going back to Longinus, he automatically knew his Savior was hanging from the Cross, Jesus was the Son of Almighty Father, in the same way as St Paul believed, soon we shall see the one we have pierced through our transgressions and immediately all will know, that He is God.

What will happen then?

You either convert or you'll be cast out, everybody has free will and as soon you are touch by that Blood and Water you'll know that He is God, but you will decide to accept Him or not, St Paul did, St Longinus did, but one who had walked beside Him from the beginning rejected Jesus… Judas.

The Illumination of Conscience will happen, that will be the second greatest act of Mercy by God the Father, the first one? When He sent His only Son to die for us in pain, humiliation and in mockery.

The Illumination of Conscience… an act of Mercy, but why wait for such beautiful act? Why can't we be like St John who believed all the way, who persevered all the way… LOVE God now with all your strength, all your heart, all your soul, so on that excellent day (Illumination of Conscience), you'll receive Love like many did when He walked the earth, Jesus Loves you and on that day it'll be a blessing, instead of crying your eyes out.

"…every eye will see him, even those who pierced him"; and all peoples on earth "will mourn because of Him." Rev 1:7

In my country there's a saying "When war is declared the soldier doesn't die by the news" so you have been warned, continue your ways: cold, lukewarm or you could decide to become hot and embrace Jesus and Jesus doesn't let you down, but rather on that day you could be lifted up, and lifted up in every sense of the word.

May you see the truth in time and live according to it, may you Love Jesus more than anything in this life, may you be a Saint in this end times and SHINE! Amen...

Soul of Mine

Soul of mine, remember who you follow, you follow Jesus of Nazareth to the heavenly homeland, remember, before that happens, you must suffer for a little while and follow everything that your Lord and Savior teaches you.

Soul of mine, remember to follow all His teachings, knowing that Maria of Divine Mercy is one of His seers and prophets, you follow her writings knowing that she is the writer and victim, Almighty Father and His only begotten Son Jesus are actually who you are really following.

Soul of mine, remember to pray for the Church, the real Pope Benedict XVI, priests, nuns, deacons, the consecrated, all the people of God, and pray for Maria of Divine Mercy with all the true prophets and visionaries that Jesus commands, what they have against them is a million times more than what you have against, so pray.

Soul of mine, you have an enemy that walks with you day and night, your flesh... for your flesh it is boring to pray, so even though your flesh, persevere, pray the Rosary, the Divine Mercy chaplet and the prayer to St. Michael the Archangel as often as you can, but do not forget the mission... pray daily the crusade prayer, sinners are in need of them.

Soul of mine, you'll be lost without the Sacraments, while they're not yet changed... have them often, especially eating, drinking and adoring the Sacred Body and Most Precious Blood of Jesus Christ your Lord before the Eucharist is canceled and the abomination of desolation is establish in the Holy Temple.

Soul of mine, when you read the messages remember the Mercy of the writer, remember to change "daughter" with you own name.

Soul of mine, remember not to mix the messages given by heaven to Maria of the Divine Mercy with other messages, be obedient, read the messages and follow His Holy word in the Bible and trust that Jesus will never leave you.

Soul of mine, remember that the Antichrist will not know Latin and your God and Savior Jesus said that there are certain aspects of the new Mass that were meant to dishonor Him, and even though Jesus did not forbid you go to the New Mass, actually you can go; but it would be wiser if you go to the Latin Mass, the Mass that brought forth the great saints of the Church, the Mass with the pleasing sacrifice without abuses in front of Almighty Father's eyes.

Soul of mine, the longer the groom to come, the more His return is delayed, more souls will be saved by your sacrifice in prayer and good example, so do not forget to pray for all sinners, don't leave the mission assigned.

Soul of mine, remember to pray for everyone, for those who have turned their backs to God, including the one who claims to be Peter, pray for him to accept Jesus Christ, do not pray for his intentions.

Soul of mine, remember that Maria of Divine Mercy is the writer, the victim, the angel of God... remember that you worship who is giving the message God, not the writer, don't fall into the trap of making false idols of her or anyone; she suffers for you, also pope Benedict XVI, as well as many other suffers for you and the conversion of souls and the final purification of the Catholic Church, watch and pray... soon, God willing, you will suffer too, as we all will be crucified with Him, so we can be Glorified in Him.

Soul of mine, souls await your prayers what are you waiting for? Go ahead, you know very well who you follow and where he is going... most ever Virgin Mary your Mother of Salvation will be there and she'll be a witness of your crucifixion beside Her sweet Son Jesus Christ. Amen

Worldliness in the Holy Temple

Today is hard to be a Catholic... a true faithful Catholic that is, many faithful are battling in their own homes, called fanatics, legalists, haters, false prophets, whitewashed tombs... loving the Lord today is hard and it is more difficult when your own Church persecutes you.

Anybody who knows the ten commandments, have read the life of our Lord and the good news of His teachings through the writings, deeds and clarifications of our Forefathers, knows what is the meaning of the word: WORLDLINESS, for those who are spiritual no definition is required and it is not our goal to give you one.

Persecution comes to those who love the Lord and wants to please Him in all He commanded, the fine line between black and white, dark and light regarding worldliness is clear as the bible has always been ALL or NOTHING, but lukewarmness is a good gray color for the world, for the devil, is just a lie sprinkled with tiny pieces of truth, but those who are spiritual... pick up what is white, black or in this case gray.

So how it is that worldliness and persecution came to be inside the Holy Temple? How it is that today some of us feel our own church has lost its way? The answer is very Large and extensive, but let us try to summarize how worldliness is ruling today in the Hierarchy of the Bride of Christ.

A plan from those who wanted to please their master, the ruler of the world, he who got in through a crack, the devil...

We all know what happened with the Vatican II council (summarizing: our Lady in Fatima told us an evil council shall be summoned), how they close the deal today? Mario Bergoglio (the pope from the end of the world) became pope, he quickly fulfilled the prophecy of St Francis of Assisi with the Franciscans of the Immaculate:

* Embraced the secular media.
* Slowly but steady seek the favor of the world (we talk too much of abortion, homosexuality and contraception...).
* Talked to millions of people through dangerous homilies and wrote a totally ambiguous and halve truth exhortation.
* Elevated many liberals to bishops, cardinals and key positions.
* Slowly removed conservatives.
* Ignored tradition every time and didn't hide his displeasure for the 2000 year tradition.

Why he embrace the world? Why he talked so many outrageous halve truths and lies ex-cathedra?

They knew what they were doing, they were getting their crowd, inside the Catholic Church and the inclusion of the world, Jews, Muslims, Gays, Divorced and remarried, Secular governments and media who likes the devil's plan of inclusion by pushing the Church to put up to date. It comes to mind 2 Thes 2:11-12

Therefore, God is sending them a deceiving power so that they may believe the lie, that all who have not believed the truth but have approved wrongdoing may be condemned.

Now what was the plan? SCHISM, they wanted to push to the ground everything sacred (and this was prophesied long ago), they wanted to have the Church for themselves and they are succeeding, this Synod of the family is my proof, all the reports leads to a schism, which they were pushing since long and God will let this happen as the wheat and the chaff has to be separated.

Worldliness has many in their grasps inside the Church, the notion that God is love and He forgives, which is true, but God doesn't condone sin and let alone let people to be proud of their sins.

Gay couples, divorce and re-married, children being let to be adopted by homosexuals, priests being prohibited to do the Latin mass, prohibited to denounce sin; it's all happening in front of our eyes, but that was intended to cast out to the desert the ones who Love the Lord in all His commandments.

Worldliness is happening in the Church and it is been cheered actively, worldliness which was planned, worldliness the rulers of the world were waiting and will applaud when this so called mercy of this false Church happens. Schism will come, schism is already among us, but it'll be proclaimed and we will have to choose between having a building or having our faith intact.

The desert awaits for us...

La Salette, Good Success, Fatima, Akita and Garabandal have alerted us, we are living in a time that soon, right after the schism this silent persecution will turn ugly, now... are you ready to be a martyr? And what do you think Benedict thinks of this worldliness? He is suffering this betrayal...

'The Holy Father will suffer much... the good will be martyred.' Our Lady in Fatima.

The desert awaits for us... are you ready to be a martyr? Or are you ready to cheer for this New False Church? Blessings...

Where is the Remnant, those who love Jesus please stand up!

Funny thing is that the schismatics are the SSPX, the enemies of the Church are the SSPX, but those merciful Germans (The German Catholic Church) are a work of art: abortive pills, no existence of hell, divorce and remarried, LGBT masses, blessings of Gay civil unions, and no respect for what is sacred like some sick joke.

Those poor Franciscans, those are the real enemy, those followers of Lefebvre, when all they wanted to do is honor the Motu propio.

And in the US is the same but with less money, a president who likes pro-life but the pope wants NO IDEOLOGY...

All over the Catholic Church those who like Orthodoxy, because they want to follow the tradition of the past, those are the enemy. Like in Costa Rica the enemies of God have declared open persecution for what is sacred, claiming UNITY, but they are so Hypocrite, by letting all others do what they want, as the Pentecostals and the enemies of God are brothers.

How far the Church has fallen? Where is the Remnant? Where are those who were born for combat? Did Leo XIII, Pope Pious XII, Pope St Pious X and all the popes of the pas t Died in vain?

WHERE ARE YOU REMNANT ARMY? THE PEARLS ARE BEEN ACTIVELY TAKEN AWAY BY THE ENEMIES OF GOD!

Jesus said: 'they became drowsy' so, the virgins who were prepared went to sleep like Peter and the sons of Thunder who slept while the enemy came to the Mount of Olives.

The Catholic Church is being taken as we speak, Bishops are talking more boldly in favor of INIQUITY and EVIL claiming that INCLUSION, UNITY and the culture of encountering one another is what God wants.

God wants for us to follow His commands despite this BEAUTIFUL false Mercy...

Where are you brothers and sisters? Will those who love their Lord RISE UP!!!

What to do? Follow Jesus commands ONLY, have the sacraments and forget about the Novus Ordo as this is the platform that will be ABUSED to the fullest, if you think Abuse has happen in the new mass, wait for this Synod to finalize.

If Jesus was persecuted so will be, persecution and martyrdom should be our goal and today many in this neo-church view traditionalists as the source of all problems, when the reality is the Gospel of Christ divides the Remnant from the false Church.

So again, where are you brothers and sisters? Will those who love Lord Jesus RISE UP!!!

Amen.

Testimony

When I was 20 years old I decided to kill myself... I had the date scheduled, for me to have a suicide.

I was popular but I found myself at the University, wasn't popular, didn't had money, didn't have a girlfriend, I hated my life...

The girl that I liked at the time convince me to go to a retreat, I went because she was going... unfortunately she didn't, she went to Spain for vacation and conspired with other friends of mine for me to go to this retreat.

I made the nuns life there difficult, those 3 days of pure mockery to everyone, but ... the day when the Holy Spirit was going to be given by imposing hands onto us... I went there just to see if there was anything out there that could give me an answer or a reason about my life...

They started to pray for me that Saturday at 8pm, September 18th 1992, I said to myself 'I feel nothing, I feel nothing, I feel..."

I began to cry like profusely, then I saw Jesus seating in a throne as big as a building, seating down staring at me and said:

"How can you do that Rafael, don't you know that I'm your King…"

I cried and cried and kept telling Him, I'm sorry, I'm sorry."

Then He disappeared… I was happy, I didn't want to die, I was actually remorseful for even thinking that…

The next day they wanted my testimony, all I said was…

"I came here dead and I'm coming out alive."

Amen.

CAN I SUE THE CHURCH?

I came in late to hear mass the other day, it takes about 20 minutes from St Petersburg to Tampa, but that is not an excuse, I came in late, did the sign of the cross, sprinkled some Holy water in my face, everyone was standing up and the priest was singing the whole mass, Latin mass that is, then I sat down and did my best to surrender myself to the supernatural atmosphere inside the Church, I remembered when I used to take catechism to get my first communion, remembered the times when I used to go to the St. Pious X chapel in Dominican

Republic with my grandmother (please do a Hail Mary for her).

Never growing up, from my parents or by my catechism did I learned about the old mass, the mass of the Saints...

I began to get upset (sad) as the priest love was noticeable with every action and word he sang, the Gregorian songs from the choir were also sang with love, sad because I discovered the Latin mass when I was 41 years old today I'm 42. It began with sadness and by the end of the mass I was angry, angry that my Church (the hierarchy) conspired to hide this mass from me.

I got to the point to start thinking? Can I sue the Church for this? No... not the Church, the clergy for their clear intentions of giving their back to God, but also omit this heavenly mass which was enjoyed by every saint born before 1960, the other mass the one I used to go (the Novus ordo), still has the Eucharist and the Word of God, but I have seen mockery, abuse and sacrilege done and today this is a normal thing.

Ask yourselves, how many father Pios, Vianneys, or deacons as St Francis of Assisi were born after the Vatican II council finished? Mother Theresa was Born in 1910, St Maria Escriva was born in 1902 and Bishop Sheen in 1895, so this modern day saints were all born when before Vatican II, can you name a powerful saint born after 1965 that is not a martyr? Precisely not one come to mind, you can see how heaven has shut the doors on our Church by their apostasy, have you seen how few priests we have and how less and less vocations come in?

Have you seen how the Franciscans of the Immaculate are being maligned and persecuted all because they wanted to do only the Latin mass and not the Novus ordo? The Franciscans of the Immaculate were the healthiest order of our Church, giving more vocations than any other order, but they were too closed minded.

This is my feud today with my Church, how they have become the new Pharisees of our times by giving their backs to God and Nascar the way the mass is celebrated, by fastening up the pace, many have fled the Church and many has apostatized; now, clarity is a luxury this days and confusion is the new gospel... I wish I could sue them all, so they can come back into their senses, but The Church has no fault of its own, but all the Judas in high places and their assistants in low places, today everything that the world desires is no longer off the table, everything is up for grabs, as the Church of Mercy, NOT the Church of Jesus, the Church of self-mercy has arrived.

Thanks Michael Voris for showing me the Latin mass, it is because Jesus wanted to happen this way for me and for you to be there at the right time, I thank you Michael Voris indeed.

Blessings...

Diabolical disorientation, the popes gave us instructions how to defeat it.

What do you think diabolical disorientation means, by definition is just that, disorientation done by the devil, but how can we see or hear when all this disorientation is around us? How distinguish truth from a lie and lie from truth...

God Almighty created us for one reason only... to love Him, to be with Him, respect Him and seek only to do what it pleases Him, He created us, so He could have a family, but then came confusion which started by satan telling Eve that God was a liar, that if they tasted the fruit from the tree then they will become gods.

Even though God Himself told them not to, they chose to hear someone else, someone who wasn't the Creator and this was the first disorientation, the first lie in the bible, the first temptation of the devil, to say that God was a liar and we all fell for it.

Jesus came to this world to break the chains of sin that bounded us to eternal damnation, through His teachings in the Gospel and through His disciples, we had everything that we needed to thrive for greatness like pope Benedict XVI once said.

The devil has done much damage in the Catholic Church and he had lots of help from Judas Iscariot his bishop, many souls have been lead stray by bad Bishops and priests during this 2000+ years of Catholicism, first we had the teachings of the Church unchanged like it supposed to be, but bit by bit the snake has found the way to sneak in and tell man: God is a liar you can be a god yourself.

Vatican II happened even though warnings from heaven that an evil council was to happen (Fatima), this council was evil because everything was left up in the air, ambiguity was done in such a way that the definition needed wasn't there, priests could interpret the council in any way they wanted... but this was also true before the council, I mean many wolves were leading stray as well.

I was watching a St. Francis of Assisi movie the other day and St, Francis wanted to preach to the Muslims and specially to the Sultan in order to stop the war, but when finally the grace of God through St. Francis hands got peace for all, they were deliberating to see if they could accept the treaty, someone said should we continue the killing? In which St. Francis said "to Kill is a sin" and a bishop there contradicted this saint and said that a peace treaty is against God's plan because a doctor and St. of the Church said that killing a Muslim was a good thing.

A doctor of the Church against one of the ten Commandments of God, this is one example of thousands, another example the protestants, in Vatican II says that they are not condemned and because of this, Ecumenism started in order so that they and everybody else felt more welcome, because a true pope sign in on that and much else, various forms of sedevacatism started.

I once spoke to one sedevacantist who told me that I was going to Hell because I was embracing the Novus Ordo and the conciliar Church, I said to her, "Excuse me what do you think of Fr. Pio?" and she said because he did the N. Ordo mass he could be in hell.

Diabolical disorientation indeed, bad catechism from the start, communion in the hand, sedevacantism, hypocrisy in our Church by most of our leaders and even by us when we are NOT catechized properly with Love.

The Novus Ordo is VALID, communion in the hand is a sin because it leads to abuse and denial of the true presence of God (see how the Vatican gives communion), NOT kneeling to receive the Holy flesh... priests, even Bishops are propagating this ERROR, sedevacantism is an error, but many don't see themselves as sedevacantists, the SSPX recognizes the power of the pope but they don't want to recognize Vatican II.

Pope Benedict had the best approach ever and it is a true sign of wisdom from heaven, Benedict welcomed the SSPX, remove the excommunications and Bishop Fellay didn't want to sign up about Vatican II, if Benedict did it this with them, he was prepared to give in something, but he also expected something in return, stop attacking Vatican II, by doing so you undermine the power of Peter.

Benedict had the right approach, I mean, you could have Latin mass, all of the graces in the teachings before the council, but stop proselyting against the Vatican II; please understand if many popes are FOR the Novus ordo, the they are FOR Vatican II and saying you can't go to a diocesan Latin mass, that you can't pray the Divine Mercy Chaplet because it was once prohibited, you are actually undermining the power of the pope and popes who reign after Vatican II, so therefore you can't say you are NOT sedevacantist when your actions speak otherwise, the Novus Ordo is VALID even though the Latin mass is superior.

Diabolical disorientation is what is going on, we need to embrace what pope Benedict XVI wanted to achieve in that meeting with Bishop Fellay, that! is the true way of Christians, the Latin mass should be given in every church, the SSPX should be with us just doing their thing protecting the beauty of tradition without undermining the power of the pope and rejecting the Novus Ordo, we shouldn't put down people because of their Christian faith BUT at the same time stand our ground with truth which is in our Church and its tradition, Catholicism is a beautiful thing a gift from Almighty Father said venerable Bishop Sheen, much ERROR is out there, but also among us because of all the wolves at the service of the devil and Judas Iscariot... tradition is very much persecuted but also traditionalists persecutes what it is VALID, is it evil, yes because we make it evil, when we don't recognize who is the Lord of Lords and the King of Kings our Savior Jesus, when we want to DO instead of letting Him do what He wants to do.

True: Protestants have damage the Church, Jews have damage the Church, Communists have damage the Church, Masons have damage the Church, Atheism has damage the Church, but the gates of hell will never prevail, yes we must stand our ground WITH the truth through the teachings and tradition of Jesus and His apostles, but do know that some of us want to embrace Christ deny the world, pick the cross up daily and follow Him, some of us can't enjoy Latin mass, some have been saved with a Divine Mercy Chaplet, some of us are converted protestants and don't understand why you kneel to a statue when the Blessed Sacrament is to the left side of the altar, most of us need unity and fraternity without renouncing truth.

John the disciple saw how someone was throwing demons out in the name of Jesus and wanted them to stop, He said that to our Lord but he said "Let them because whoever loves me can't speak ill of me."

But because of much abuse over the centuries, Protestantism occurred and they took many souls stray, but how about those who had gone in the jungles were Catholicism never has been, converted many and died for their faith, died for the Gospel, are they in hell? Of course not, they embraced Christ, all this Christians... Coptic, Orthodox been martyred in Africa, are they in hell? No! Don't judge the book by its cover.

There are many contradictions that lead to disorientation, many traditionalists say Mother Theresa of Calcutta wasn't good because she was among the idolaters, have we become Pharisees all over again? Divine Mercy Chaplet is no good? Wao! Saint Liguori dealt with Jews, he had lots of Mercy with them, did he became a Jew? No... did Mother Theresa became shiva? No! We need to drop our masks and thrive for greatness like Pope Benedict XVI said, and crush the diabolical disorientation with the Rosaries and the Chaplet, like John Paul II would've wanted.

Forgive me for all this words, I'm against Hypocrisy, because I've been a Hypocrite most of my life but I want to throw myself to the feet of my Lord and thrive for greatness, me the most miserable worm out there, I want heaven through Jesus Mercy.

Pope St. John Paul II, pray for us

THE WAY TO THE GOLGOTHA

He was walking towards a man who asked:

-"Are you catholic"

"Yes I am" he replied, he wasn't expecting what was coming, he thought he was in a friendly community, then a slap in the face and laughter brought him to reality, he went down to the ground, and after a while he realize what was going on, he stood up, went to the same guy again and showed him the other cheek... Immediately with anger and fury this huge man began to beat him down, it wasn't a slap only, punches and kicks were given and the first drop of blood touched the ground...

Catholic: "May my blood be of help for you to get saved."

Then he took his rosary out and while kneeling began to pray the rosary for the salvation of that man and all around him, people in shock stood froze and the man became more violent when he showed him a large construction wood stick...

-"So you're better than me, better than all the rest...?"

He did not replied he continued counting his beads, when he was struck in the head with the stick which opened his head and much blood came down... but he didn't move, it was like nothing happened to him, much blood was coming down... the people around started to kneel down to pray the rosary too, while an old lady came to put a gauze on this man's head...

When he saw that all were praying a tear came down from his left eye, the abuser's mother was among the praying people, he kneel and asked God for forgiveness...

Many people right now all over the world is being persecuted, some are the victims that heaven needs to bring to righteousness the sinners, some others are martyrs whose blood is spilled to cleanse the church... many are killed in unspeakable ways, others raped, others slaved, others chopped like for the fun of an audience; tears and blood meet.

Jesus, is taking part in this new beating, this horrors are His, because He is the Master and Teacher, no one has suffered like He did, so... He must teach you to carry your cross to the Golgotha, but He never leaves you alone in this path, He... after a while, you will see Him carrying the cross with you and sharing your pain, which doesn't hurt like before, now watching the Master is worthwhile, His smile puts you almost in heaven, and when the time comes, you'll reach the top of the Hill with Him...

There, He will give you another miracle, as John listened the sweet sound of His Merciful Heart, you will too hear the Melodious sound of the waves of Mercy for you and the world, He will put you down to sleep like a Father does to His precious princess, put you in bed, which is the cross to sleep for a little while... Then you'll say:

"I wasn't worthy but you taught me to be yours, so please remember me when you come in to your Kingdom", and the lasts words you'll hear *"Amen I say to you, today you will be with me in paradise."*

The good pain of Christ, those by His friends who please Him in all His commands, those pains are His, because He never leaves you alone in this path of righteousness, which hurts so much, His tears will encounter yours; since His death and resurrection all the pain of the ones that are His flock, that pain is His, you are not alone walking to the Golgotha.

His friends have walked with Him and suffered with Him, giving the Gospel by example and voice, many have believe because of those going to the Golgotha to share the good pains that only gives you glory in Him.

The most horrendous pain is the one that he shares with "no one", the pain that is inflicted upon Him by the people that are supposed to know Him, treason makes His sweat fall like blood on the ground.

Judas walked the earth with Him, saw Lazarus come out of the grave, saw lepers cleanse out of their miseries, he saw when Jesus walked upon the waters, Judas saw many evil spirits go out screaming from men, he went out with the 72 and proselytized, but instead took the 30 silver coins.

Many have seen small miracles and big ones as well, but they rather sell the Gospel, they have studied the lives of the saints and the teachings of our forefathers, but instead prefer some other strange teachings...

Thomas More died because Henry the VIII wanted to divorce his legitimate wife and re-marry, so because of this king, a traitor, Saint Thomas More was decapitated and his pains were with Jesus, the majority of the Bishops nailing Jesus to the cross again like Pharisees happened, and the procession to the Golgotha went with pure hatred for the sacred, instead the gain of power was placed, their own 30 silver coins.

The bad pains, the ones that makes Jesus suffered the stripes of open flesh, the thorns to the skull and one to His sweet eye... the big cross with all the spitballs and mockery, until the nails go in once again.

Proselytism brought us Saint Thomas More and many martyrs, St John the Baptist is weeping as many in silence are behaving like Herod, proselytism have brought the many who have shared the good pains with our Lord…

Today we need to make a decision, are we going to let the Lord taught us the way to the Golgotha and be a good disciple, or are we going to get our 30 silver coins…

Catholics were born for greatness, said pope Benedict XVI and this greatness lies in the cross which is hold by the nails impale to our flesh, proselytism is a good thing, Catholicism is a beautiful thing, when we give ourselves to Jesus the Master and Teacher... Don't let anybody deceive you, Jesus is that Catholic God and I believe in a Catholic God, and I hope you do too.

Blessings in our Lord Jesus Amen

Lastly...

My path to sainthood is indeed a rocky one, I'm not there yet... but make no mistake, we are destined for greatness said our sweet pope Benedict XVI and that greatness lies, not in our own strength, but in our blind trust in Jesus.

"If you Love Me you will keep my commandments."
John 14:15

I use to be just another misled child of God, misled by the devil and its dominion: the world, the world rejoices with those who are their property.

I have been lied since day one, in so many ways that it is hard for me to trust just in any of those "truths" the world present today, but sure did since day one...

There is only one truth and that truth is Jesus, now my enemy, my flesh... makes me stumble, fall, to reach out to my Lord each and every time, I have little control for what my flesh desires, but the saints did managed to control their flesh throughout their lives, I sure hope for that control one day...

Please bear with me a little bit as I try to explain who I am and what I'm trying to do...

The first time I felt Jesus it was in my heart, my school send us to a day of retreat somewhere in 1990 and while at confession, felt Him for the first time, a holy priest put his hand in my chest, right where my heart is, he closed his eyes and said to me:

"Jesus loves you, loves you, loves you very much."

My poor heart got in flames, literally in flames... that burning was unexpected, at the time I've never felt something like that, so supernatural, so beautiful, but I wasn't prepared to embrace that much beauty and it faded away after months, thanks to my apathy.

I fell, slowly, deep into darkness... 2 years later, as my memories of Jesus were dormant, buried in my oblivious mind, I wanted to take my life, I planned to kill myself by the 22nd of November 1992; yes it was the usual, no love, no money, nothing going my way and worst of all, thought that I would go to a better place, as the fiery picture of hell, I did not believe in.

I got tricked by my friends to go into a Catholic retreat, there, on September the 19th they imposed hands upon my head and pray for the Holy Spirit to bless me with His Love...

At the beginning I kept saying:

"I feel nothing, I feel nothing..."

All of the sudden I was crying like a child, then...He was there, I saw Him, Jesus...

Everything was gone, nothing existed anymore, it was only me and Jesus, He was bigger than the tallest building in the world, had His crown of Thorns, white robe, He was seating on His Throne, then He said to me:

"How can you do that Rafael? Don't you know I am your King?"

My Lord was referring about my suicidal intentions, all I kept saying to Him was: "I'm sorry, I'm sorry." Then He disappeared, on that day (September 19th 1992), I was born again.

I didn't told anyone in my house at the time, my intent to end my life was gone, but, I let the door open for the world, my romance with the Lord passed and the matters of daily life took over.

Eventually I found my way to a youth charismatic group, there I found my future wife, sincerely, we did what we thought was our Lord's wishes, yes we preached, we try to save souls, but my time there, despite that, it was kind of lukewarmth...

There, I was called to become a priest and I had my future wife with me, I'd fought my Lord every second, to do my will and not His.

After me and my love one parted ways with much hurting, I went to the Passionist seminary in 1996, I loved my girlfriend very much so I struggled with the idea, but my Lord was calling, Fr. Angel was surprised to see me there and started my days as a seminarian.

During those months I grew a little bit, I was so immature in life, I still am...

There I listen to my Lord for the first time in years, we were given a task, to pray to the Lord in front of the tabernacle and write anything on a piece of paper, I said to Jesus:

"You are beautiful my Lord."

And Jesus responded, to my surprise, He said:

"What is beautiful, is Almighty Father..."

When I read those words to the priest, he said to me in front of all other seminarians:

"That it's just what people say to be praised by others."

I didn't reply back, even though I wasn't trying to be praised, because I've always been an attention seeker, even though… this time, I wasn't looking for attention.

All throughout my life I'd always craved for the praise of the world, attention, even pity, just to get noticed, I guess I just wanted to be loved; attention is so appealing to me, is still is... a temptation, I struggle with humility... the love of anyone in the World, my struggle.

Bear with me, I mean... before the seminary I wanted to become a doctor, a doctor for all the wrong reasons, you see... my Father had a private office, an internist, a cardiologist in New York city, made more than a million dollars while practicing, when dollars were dollars, the Dominican community respected him and having 60 patients a day was an everyday thing.

My Father divorced my Mother when I was little and re-married in an Evangelical Church, had 4 children more, I wanted to be like him... respected, loved by his community and rich.

Eventually the prayers of my Mother were heard in heaven, she asked for Justice, my father treated my mother like garbage when together, Justice did came... my dad lost everything, he was charged with a federal crime, charged as a part of a 30 million dollar scheme which robbed Medicare.

To tell you the truth he wasn't the mastermind, but the one who did the con, made a deal with the FBI and gave up many doctors... including my father.

My father, Dr. Rafael Gonzalez Pantaleon was guilty, he knew something was wrong, but failed to report it in time and did enjoy the scrapes of a scheme he didn't knew it was, he didn't understood it well, took the money but didn't report to the authorities what was going on.

My father was found guilty, but eluded the authorities when he fled to the Dominican Republic where no extradition was implemented for such a crime, only narcotics could warrant extraditions.

My father crave for money was his downfall, both in New York and in the Dominican Republic, he tried to go to another country and make money there, the FBI caught him in Europe and did his time in a Massachusetts prison.

Anyways...

After I left the seminary, did amends with my ex-girlfriend and got married, the whole arrest of my father happened in Dominican Republic, it was all too public at the time, I was trying to become a doctor... once again, I forgot about Jesus.

Six Years of Med School, 3 beautiful children, an awesome wife... a good life, but forgot the love of my life, my Savior Jesus Christ. I was preparing to take the boards in order to practice where I was born: the United States.

I was a pretty good doctor, I used to correct professors, doctors who had practice medicine for decades... I was feared, I became what I hated as student, one of those who knew it all.

Unfortunately there wasn't time for Jesus in my successful student life... until death, came knocking at my door.

I remember that night like it was yesterday, It was a cold night, a long day after my pediatrics internship round was due, as I laid down in bed, I felt that there was something wrong and went to sleep, the next morning I was sick, I thought that I've catch a cold and went home, there, I became sicker and sicker, the days went by, took Tylenols for the fever but the temperature wasn't going away, so I started to take a fever reduction medicine called

Neomelubrina, a pill that has as a side effect... bone marrow suppression.

The bone marrow is the one responsible to create red cells and white cells in the body, the red cells can have a lifespan of 120 days in the body, white cells are constantly created to battle bacteria, viruses and with that gone, you can imagine my struggle with infections.

After days, nothing was getting me better and the doctors didn't had a clue, I didn't had a clue as I thought I had dengue fever and the blood works were inconclusive from the start, then they've found I had pneumonia, but nobody could pinpoint my issues with the neomelubrina, which killed my defenses, the infection caused my lungs to collapsed, I had to be induced into a drug coma with intubation so I could breathe.

I knew I was going to die when they told me that I was going to be induced into coma, I started to fight the doctors, nurses, my colleagues physically...

When I couldn't stopped them any longer, I knew it was the end, so I prayed:

"Lord Jesus, I'm sorry I didn't do much for You as You would've want me to, please, if someone from heaven is coming to get me, let 'Madrina' (my grandmother's sister) be the one who take me."

I closed my eyes into unconsciousness and bad news were given to my family daily, my wife couldn't stop crying, both of my sisters came from the countries where they lived, only to receive bad news after bad news, remember, doctors didn't had a clue what I had.

My basic problem was that even though I took neomelubrina for myself, when I got to the hospital, the doctors continued to give me that drug, even though my bone marrow was deteriorating, eventually they found out later and took that drug out of my regimen.

People started to hear about my case and by the word of mouth people prayed for me, all over the world, prayer was offered for my recovery... my mother damage both of her knees praying, my wife cried for days and she gave me to my Lord saying:

"Please Jesus, he is yours, if you have to take him... do so, but don't let him suffer."

Two different people saw Jesus taking care of me while in coma, at my bed and through many other testimonies, my family kept receiving good news from the King of Kings.

After 7 days in coma I woke up, thinking that only one day has passed, not thinking that I almost died twice in those 7 days, people were thinking and talking about my funeral arrangements.

Bilateral several pneumonia, acute kidney failure due to septic shock, bone marrow suppression which caused an aplastic anemia, my family kept praying and their prayer was answered... I was alive.

Struggled much, I had to learn how to walk again... my muscles became atrophic in just 7 days, we had a gigantic medical bill, my dad in prison, no money and later we got a surprise, my trachea was collapsing, after I got out of the hospital my trachea suffered a collapse of 90%... it is called trachea stenosis.

My doctor advised me to go to the United States, as laser in the Dominican Republic was an issue, because my Island (Dominican Republic), didn't had one... so if I needed some laser I could be out of luck.

My Sister was doing Internal Medicine at Mercy Hospital in Queens NY, I got there and started my treatment, Dr. Michael Korst did my 1st surgical procedure and later, major surgery at the Weil-Cornell Presbyterian Hospital, but it didn't work...

My slow path to recovery, the many surgeries (more than 15), with many setbacks, my surgeon had a tough time keeping my trachea from collapsing, the books I studied says that If the 1st major surgery doesn't heal this type of problem (trachea stenosis), then it was hard to heal later on and that's precisely what happened.

All my surgeries I tried to have a positive mind, thinking that God, who save me from a certain death, would take care of me, I was certain that I was going to get better.

After my 2nd surgery I felt sick, I was feeling hot, with a fever and I went to bed that afternoon, the Lord appeared to me in my dreams, He said:

"This is what I want you to do, I want you to speak about My Mercy to the whole world and as a proof of this… tomorrow there will be no light."

My only response was:

"Lord I have a fever"

He looked at me and said…

"Don't worry, I will take care of this"

Next Morning I woke up amazed about this dream, I had no fever and I thought to myself that today we would have a blackout... instead a miracle...

THE HEAVENS WERE COVERED WITH DARK CLOUDS, THERE WAS NO LIGHT!!!

My Father called from prison in Boston and I didn't share this dream with him at the time, I asked Him how the sky was there, he said:

"The sky is black"

My wife from Dominican Republic called, 1500 miles from Hempstead, New York and I asked her the same question without her knowing this dream, she said:

"The sky is pitch black with a lot of thunders"

After I told her about my dream she felt scared, I was too, because of this big job given to me by Jesus, my rocky path begins... I love you Jesus!

www.ingramcontent.com/pod-product-compliance
Lightning Source LLC
Chambersburg PA
CBHW051815090426
42736CB00011B/1488